Famous Illustrators of the Golden Age
Coloring Portfolio ™

Famous Illustrators of the Golden Age Coloring Portfolio
©2022 Joe Lacey

ISBN: 979-8-9863300-3-7   Second Edition

Sources used in the research of biographical text:
Adams, Henry "Wyeth's World," Smithsonian, 2006. / BettyCrocker.com, The Betty Crocker Portraits, January 10, 2017. / Duncan, Alastair, Art Nouveau (World of Art), Thames & Hudson, 1994. / Kitch, Carolyn, The Girl on the Magazine Cover: The Origins of Visual Stereotypes in American Mass Media, Univ. of North Carolina Press, 2001. / Meyer, Susan E., James Montgomery Flagg, Watson-Guptill, 1974. Peterson, William S., The Beautiful Poster Lady: A Life of Ethel Reed, Oak Knoll Press, 2013. / "Press Release." The National Museum of American Illustration. July 5, 2006. / Prieto, Laura R., At Home in the Studio: The Professionalization of Women Artists in America. Harvard University Press, 2001. / Reed, Walt and Roger, The Illustrator in America 1880-1980, Madison Square Press, Inc., 1984. / "Sarah Stilwell Weber (Cover Artists)." The Saturday Evening Post. January 7, 2015. /Schau, Michael, All-American Girl: The Art of Coles Phillips, Watson-Guptill, 1975.

Famous Illustrators of the Golden Age

The Golden Age of Illustration is a period in time in America from the 1880s–1920s when paintings and drawings adorned the covers of magazines and appeared on posters and advertisements. Technical advancements in commercial printing were evolving, bringing more vibrant colors and fine details never before imagined. These illustrations created by highly talented artists, many in their youth and just starting careers in art, helped to entertain the public, sell products, and chronicle day-to-day life. So important was this art, many of these illustrators became household names and lived lifestyles of fame and fortune not dissimilar to modern day movie or music stars. Born in or immigrated to America, these artists were influenced by the Romantic, Art Nouveau, and Art Deco movements of Europe. Taking inspiration from all three, these artists created a uniquely American genre of art. It was an exciting and imaginative time in history with influences that are felt to this day.

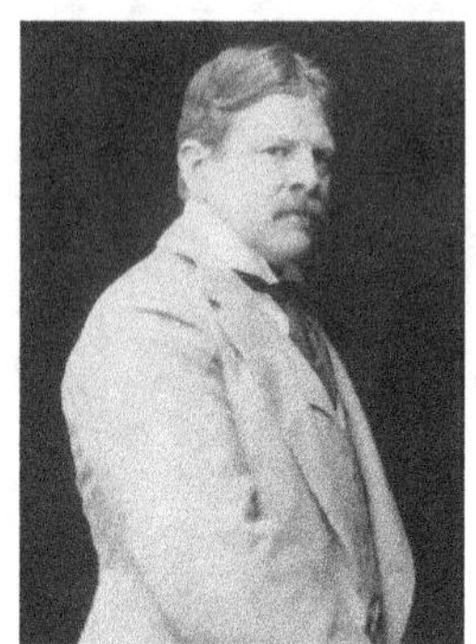

Edwin Austin Abbey *(April 1, 1852 – August 1, 1911)* began his illustration career during the Golden Age of Illustration when mass magazine printing was just evolving. He lived much of his life in England, where he had access to authentic costumes, props, and locations for his paintings of historical and Shakespearean subjects. His murals can be seen at the Boston Public Library and Pennsylvania State Capitol. His series of murals entitled *The Quest and Achievement of the Holy Grail* took eleven years to complete.

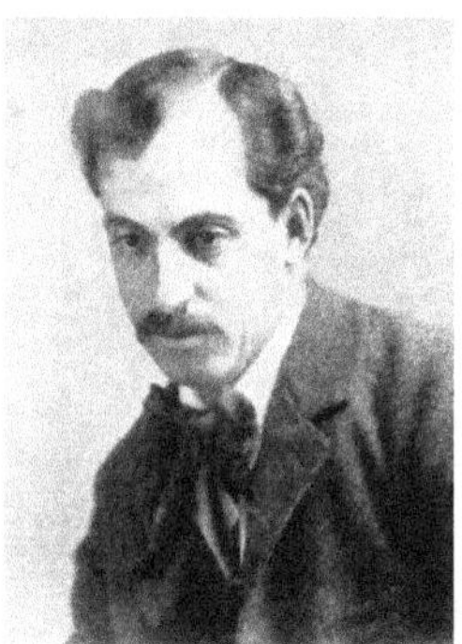

Will H. Bradley *(July 10, 1868 – January 25, 1962)* with his fanciful and highly detailed artwork was the definition of a designer-illustrator. He incorporated typography, stylized imagery, and graphics in his posters and books. He was the leading Art Nouveau illustrator of his time. He is credited for popularizing the flat graphic approach to posters in the United States, often with elements of Arts & Crafts sensibilities. He was a writer, film maker, art director, publisher, and type designer.

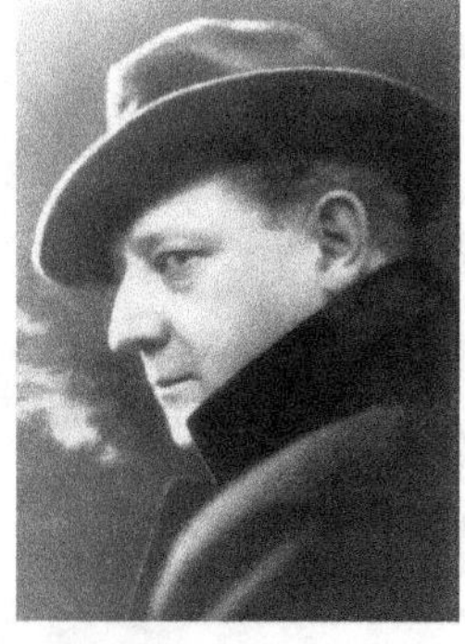

Harrison Fisher *(July 27, 1875 or 1877 – January 19, 1934)* is known for his delicate drawings and paintings of beautiful women. His subjects are often depicted wearing large hats and surrounded by flowers. They are placed in scenes of romance and upper class society. His illustrations adorned most of the popular magazines of the time. He also illustrated books and created posters for the American Red Cross. Under an exclusive contract with *Cosmopolitan*, Fisher painted over 300 covers for the magazine.

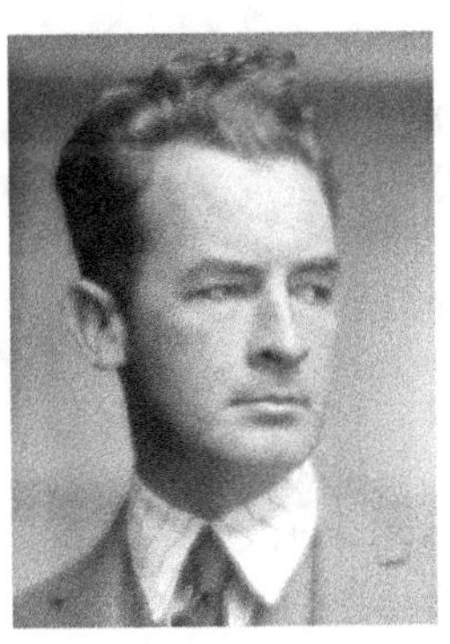

James Montgomery Flagg (*June 18, 1877 – May 27, 1960*) was a master of many mediums and genres — from illustration and fine art to satirical cartooning. His energetic pen & ink work is considered some of the finest examples of the medium. His illustrations appeared on the covers and pages of top magazines, including *LIFE, Cosmopolitan, Vanity Fair,* and *Judge.* He is most well known for his political posters of WWI and WWII. His 1917 *I Want You* poster for the U.S. Army is one of the most recognizable images in American history. Flagg himself posed as Uncle Sam for this and other political posters.

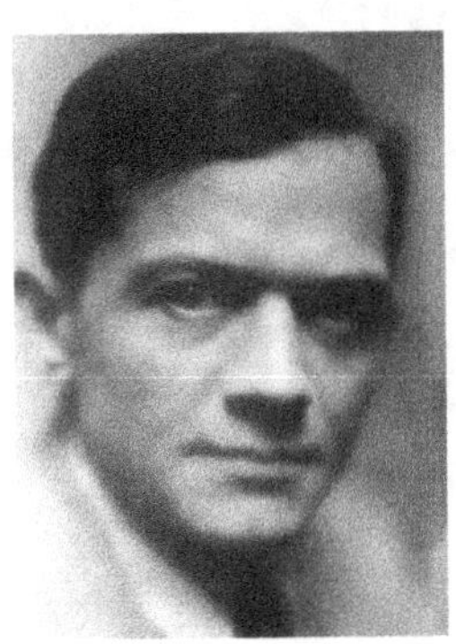

John Held Jr. (*January 10, 1889 – March 2, 1958*) was an illustrator who defined the Jazz Age of the 1920s with his cartoons of flappers, jazz bands, college life, and the world of socialites. His illustrations are highly stylized and have a bold Art Deco approach. The majority of his commercial work was for magazines and books. His most famous book cover is for *Tales of the Jazz Age* by author F. Scott Fitzgerald. During the Great Depression, his work fell out of favor, and Held moved on to breeding and sculpting horses.

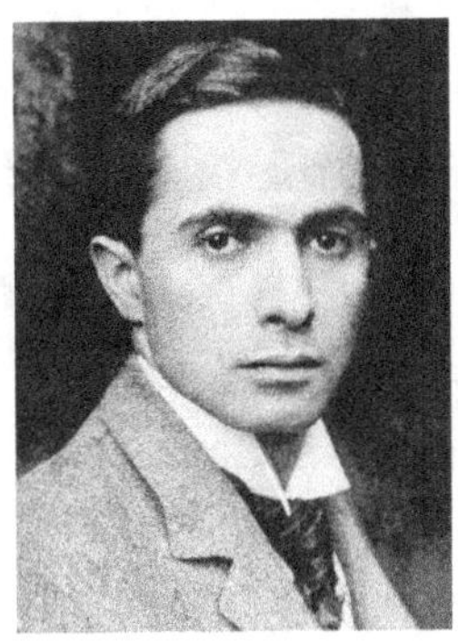

J. C. Leyendecker (*March 23, 1874 – July 25, 1951*) laid the groundwork for the look of the modern advertisement and magazine cover with his illustration and design sensibilities. He painted 322 covers for *The Saturday Evening Post,* most famously his "New Year's Baby" series. He created many advertising campaigns for Kellogg's Corn Flakes and The House of Kuppenheimer. He is the creator of the Arrow Collar Man, a sophisticated, handsome symbol of male fashion. So effective were his ads, women wrote love letters not to Leyendecker, but to the Arrow Collar Man. His work was a major influence on Norman Rockwell.

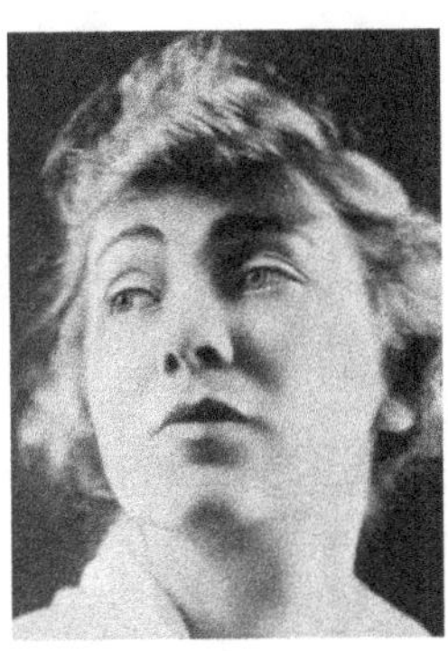

Neysa McMein (*January 24, 1888 – May 12, 1949*) illustrated numerous ads for leading publishers of the time. She was the exclusive cover illustrator for *McCall's* from 1923–1937, creating over 168 covers for the magazine. Many of her early illustrations were done with pastels, but she was also an accomplished portrait painter. In 1936 she created the first portrait for General Mills' fictional cooking expert Betty Crocker which was in use for nearly 20 years. McMein was an active supporter of women's rights and the women's suffrage movement.

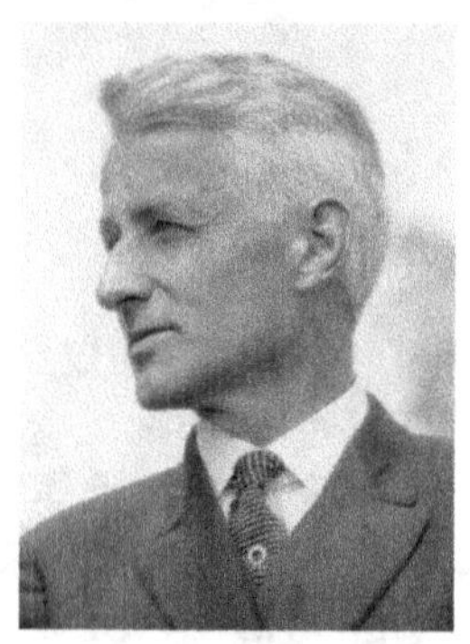

Maxfield Parrish *(July 25, 1870 – March 30, 1966)* is best known for his fantasy images of people, castles, and landscapes. He painted with a glazing technique that overlaid numerous levels of thin oil paint, creating a luminous and vibrant appearance. He is so synonymous with this method that the rich blues in his paintings are referred to as "Parrish blue." He often employs the use of "dynamic symmetry," a design theory that uses a system of lines and grids to balance the picture while at the same time creating movement and energy. In 1925, twenty-five percent of American homes had one of his prints hanging on their walls. His painting *Daybreak* was the most popular art print of the 20th century.

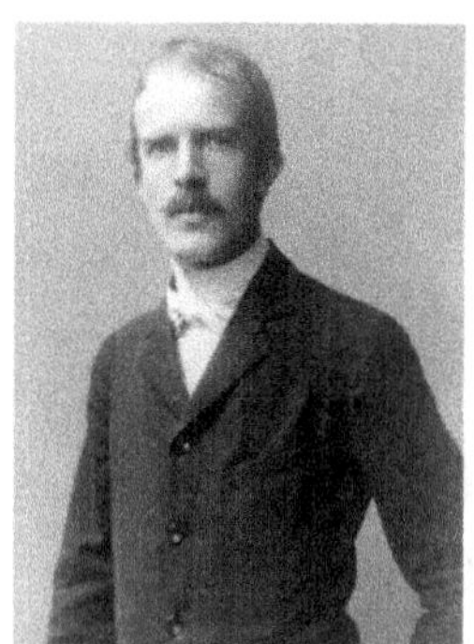

Edward Penfield *(June 2, 1866 – February 8, 1925)* was a book, magazine, and poster designer whose style is similar to French Post-Impressionist Toulouse-Lautrec. His work is purposely simple and uses expressive bold brush lines. He believed that "A design that needs study is not a poster, no matter how well executed." A favorite subject of his was scenes depicting men and women enjoying the good life, often engaged in sporting events or riding horse drawn carriages and driving automobiles.

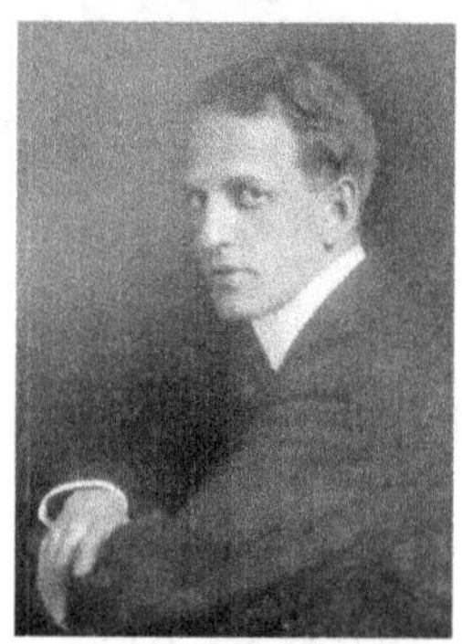

Coles Phillips *(October 3, 1880 – June 13, 1927)* is best known for his stylized "fade-away girl" which incorporates negative space to complete the shape of his subject. The designs often include a fully rendered head, arms, and hands with a flat, solid toned treatment of clothing and backgrounds. He helped popularize the Art Deco style in America with his use of geometric shapes and strong colors. He painted with watercolor on large upright surfaces, something not common to watercolorists. His paintings were often twice the size as they appeared in print for magazines and books.

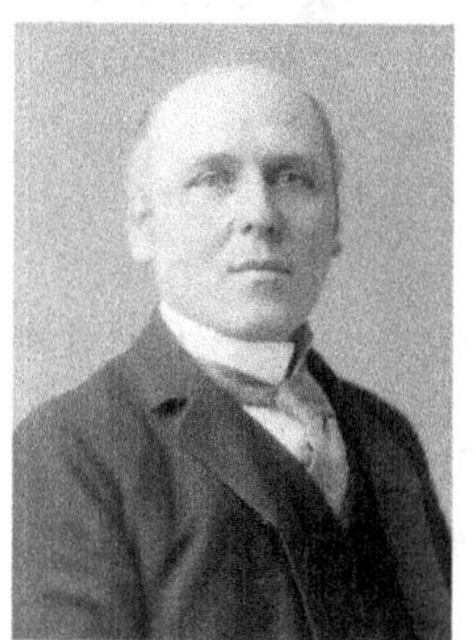

Howard Pyle *(March 5, 1853 – November 9, 1911)* is a painter and instructor referred to as the "Father of American Illustration." He wrote and illustrated children's books, including *The Merry Adventures of Robin Hood, Men of Iron,* and *The Wonder Clock.* His illustrations from *Howard Pyle's Book of Pirates,* depicting swashbuckling pirates in flowing robes and dangling earrings, are responsible for the modern day pirate seen in Hollywood movies. He founded the Brandywine School in 1900, an artists colony in Wilmington, Delaware and Chadds Ford, Pennsylvania, where he trained illustrators in the craft and business of art. Some of his students included Jessie Willcox Smith, N. C. Wyeth, Elizabeth Shippen Green, and Sarah Stilwell Weber.

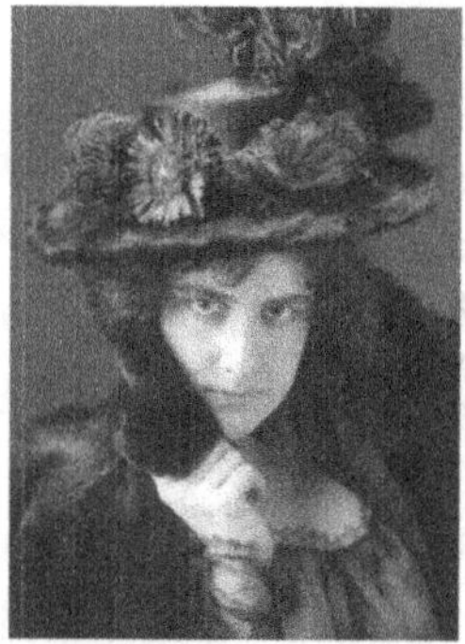

Ethel Reed *(March 13, 1874 – 1912)* achieved fame and success at an early age. She became a sought after artist at the age of eighteen, and her Art Nouveau-style poster designs made her one of the best known woman artists of the 1890s. She was the subject of Boston gossip columnists, and Reed reveled in her newfound media celebrity. In 1897 she left America to live in England where she worked for several years, but soon abandoned her short career.

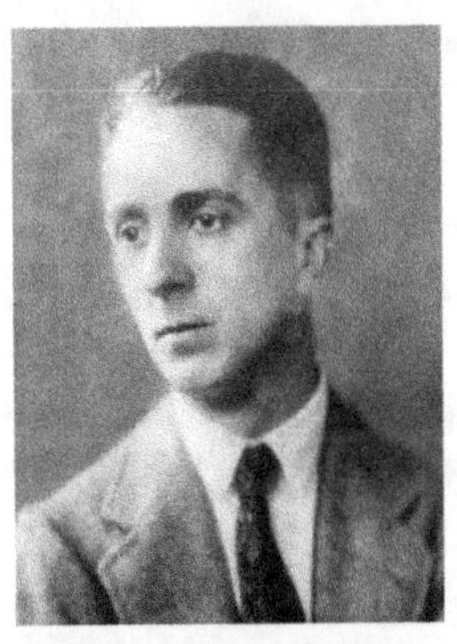

Norman Rockwell *(February 3, 1894 – November 8, 1978)* is synonymous with the real and romanticized depiction of American life portrayed on more than 300 *The Saturday Evening Post* covers. He produced over 4,000 pieces of art ranging from magazine illustrations, advertisements, posters, murals, and portraits, some of which hang in the White House. His 1943 series *The Four Freedoms* is his most famous work of art and was used during WWII to sell millions of dollars in war bonds. Many of his original works can be seen today at the Norman Rockwell Museum in Stockbridge, Massachusetts.

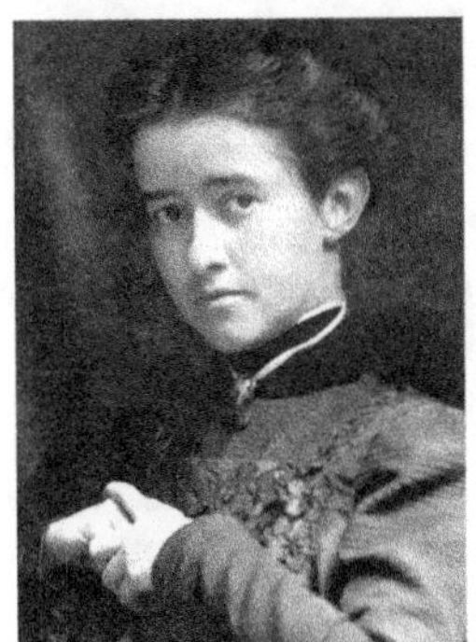

Elizabeth Shippen Green *(September 1, 1871 – May 29, 1954)* is a magazine illustrator known for her use of vibrant color and delineated line treatment. She was a student of Howard Pyle and worked with Jessie Willcox Smith and painter Violet Oakley. The three were known as "The Red Rose Girls," referring to the Red Rose Inn where they maintained a working studio. The emergence of women partaking in professional illustration was a part of the "New Woman" movement of the late 19th century in which women sought more independent and active roles in society.

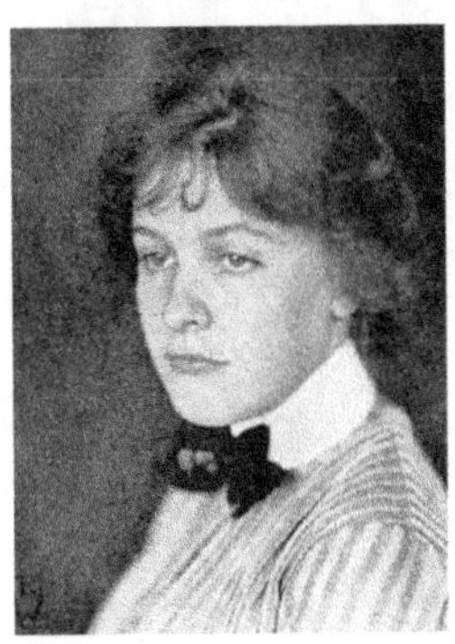

Sarah Stilwell Weber *(September 15, 1877 – April 6, 1939)* was one of the first women illustrators to have artwork on the cover of *The Saturday Evening Post*. Between 1904 and 1925, she illustrated sixty of the magazine's covers. Prior to 1904, only men were hired as illustrators. As a student of Howard Pyle, she painted in a realistic and traditional manner. Eventually her work became more stylized, with figures that meld in to one another with curving forms and highly decorative patterns.

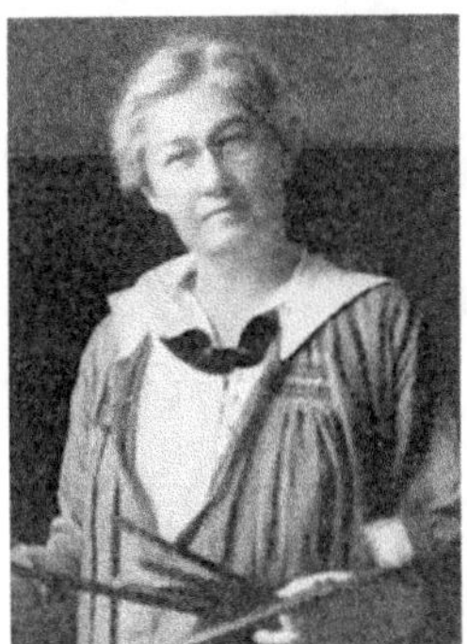

Jessie Willcox Smith *(September 6, 1863 – May 3, 1935)* is one of the most famous women illustrators. A student of Howard Pyle, she created artwork for magazines, books, advertisements, and posters. Many of her paintings combine mixed media techniques of oil, watercolor, pastels, gouache, or charcoal. From December 1917 through April 1933, her artwork appeared on every cover of *Good Housekeeping*. She illustrated more than sixty books for children. Her best known are *A Child's Garden of Verses, The Jessie Willcox Smith Mother Goose,* and *The Water Babies*.

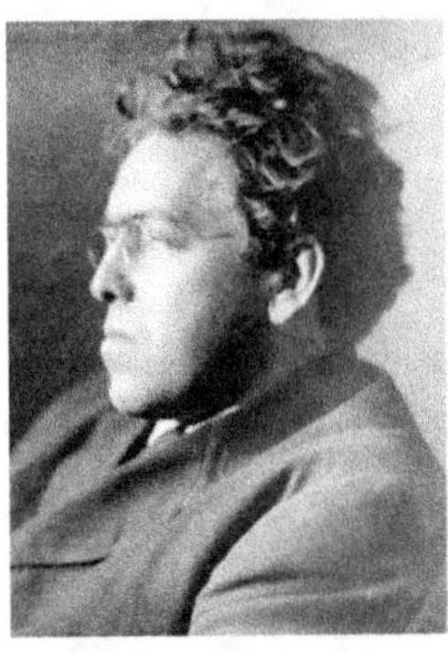

N. C. Wyeth *(October 22, 1882 – October 19, 1945)* is one of America's greatest illustrators. A student of Howard Pyle, he created more than 3,000 paintings and illustrated over 100 books. His career began with painting primarily western pictures for magazines. He later moved to illustrating classic literature and was able to purchase his home and studio with the money earned from his first book commission, *Treasure Island.* Throughout his life he painted everything from posters, calendars, advertisements, and murals to fine art. His paintings can seen at the Brandywine River Museum of Art in Chadds Ford, Pennsylvania.

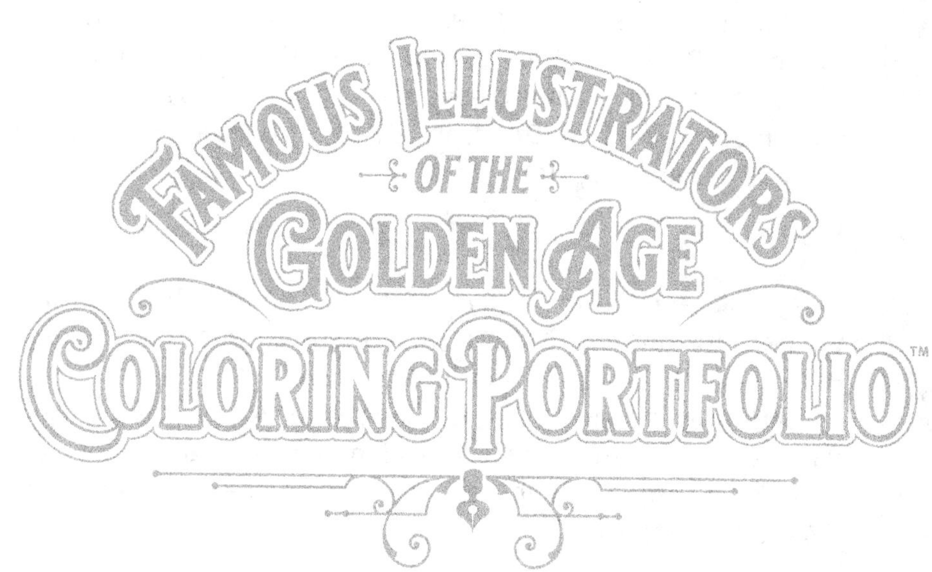

J.C. Leyendecker – 1924. Kuppenheimer Good Clothes.

Sarah Stilwell Weber – 1916. *Woman with leopard.*

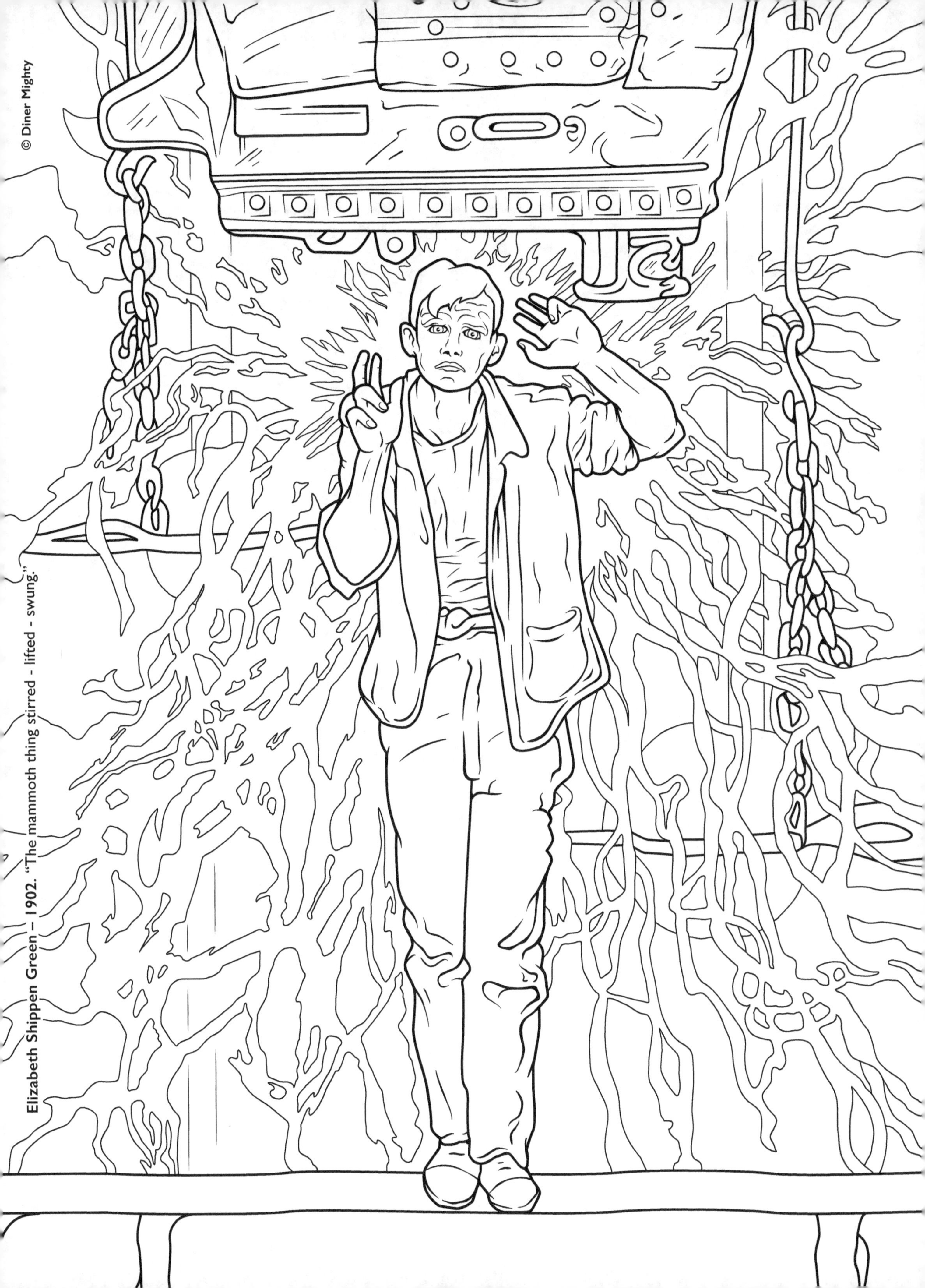

Elizabeth Shippen Green — 1902. "The mammoth thing stirred – lifted – swung."

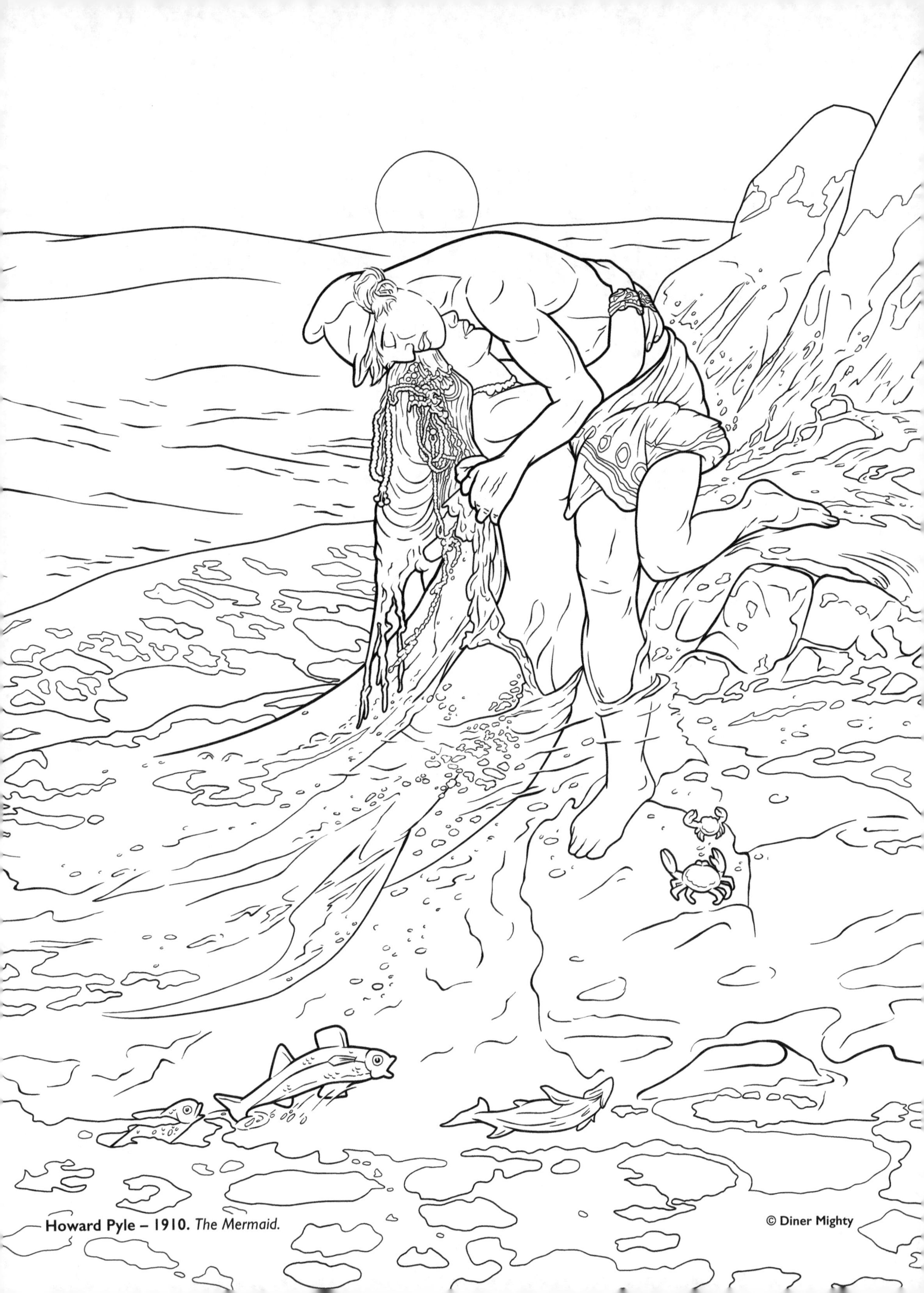

Howard Pyle – 1910. *The Mermaid.*

© Diner Mighty

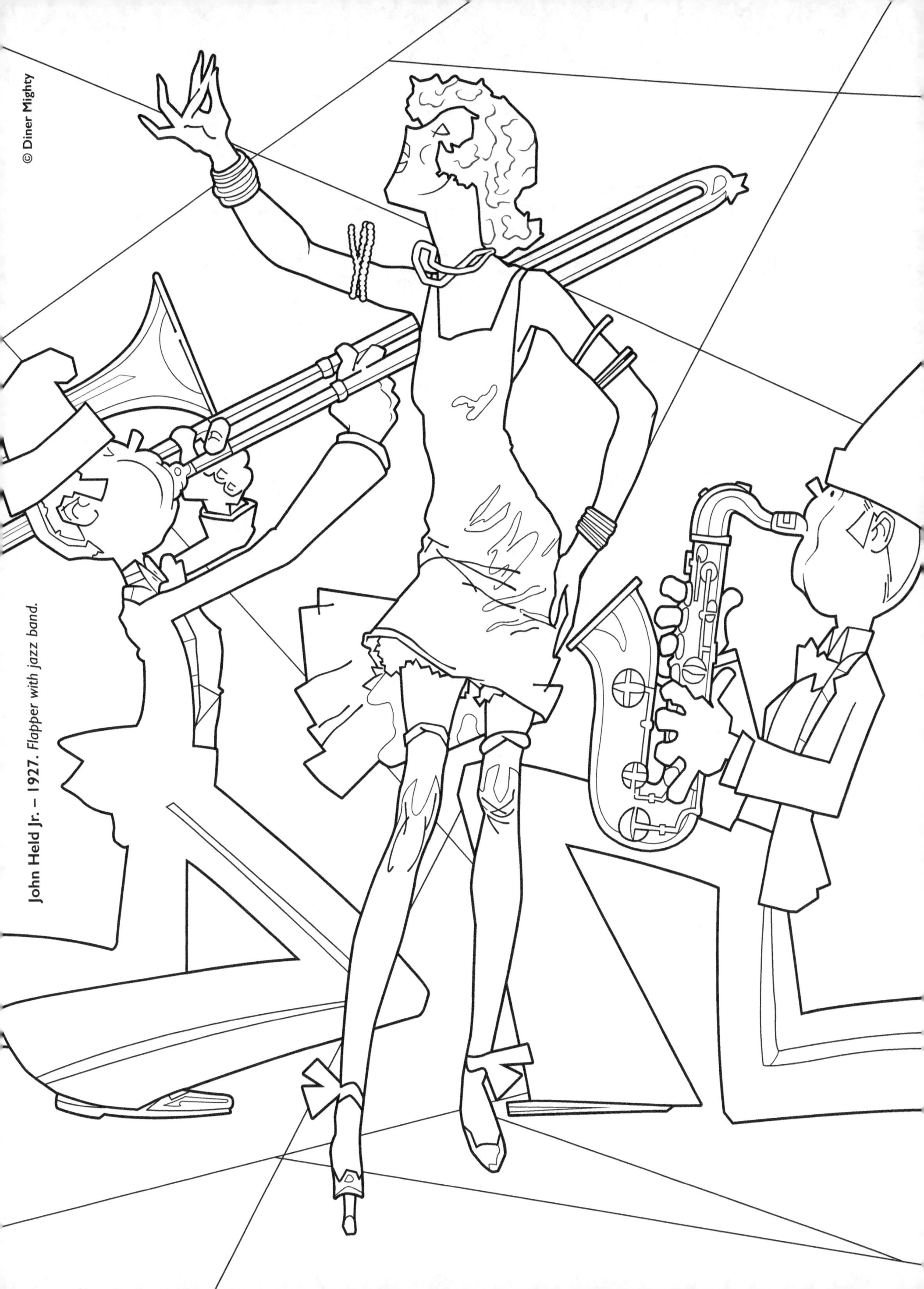

John Held Jr. – 1927. Flapper with jazz band.

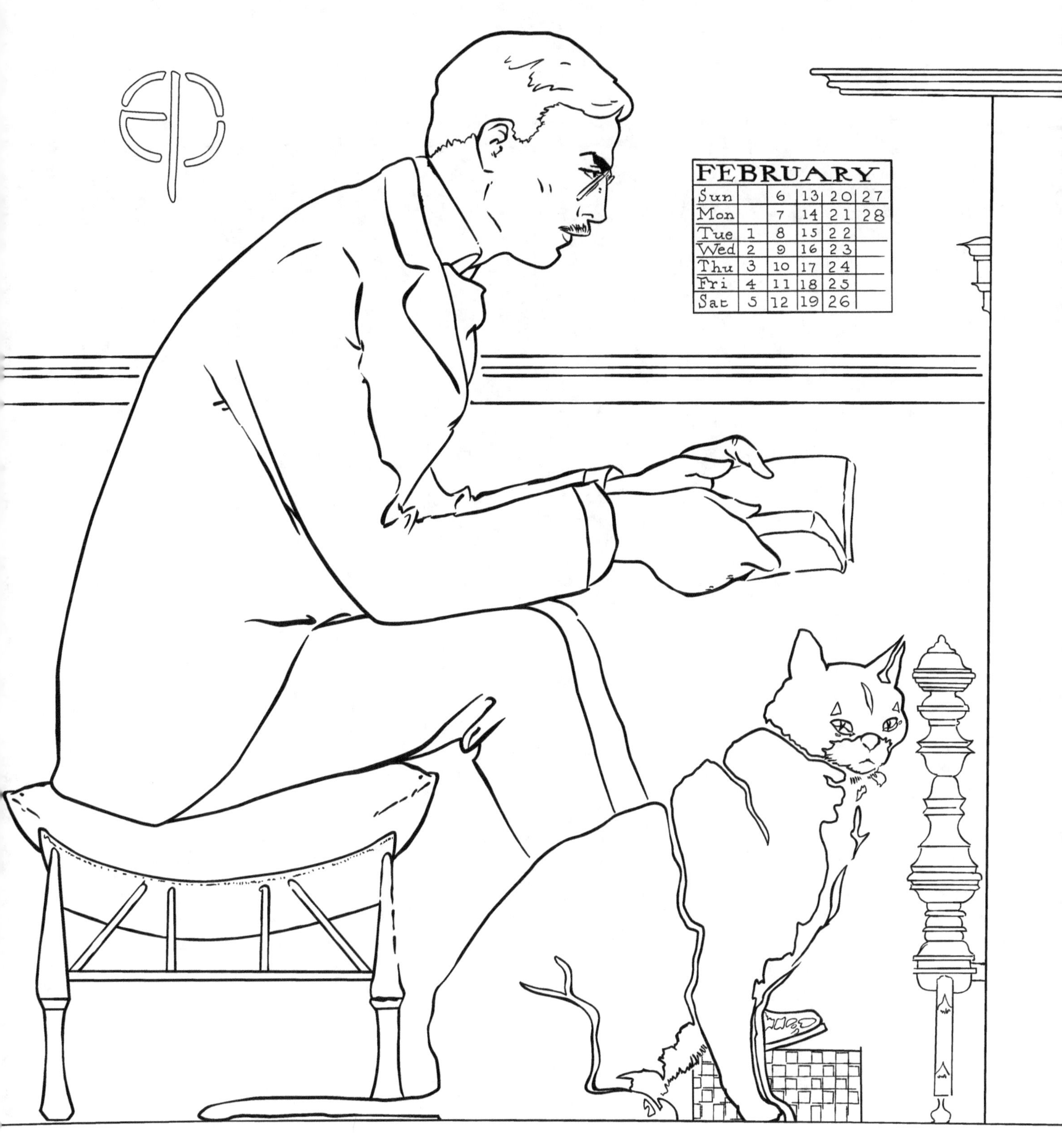

Edward Penfield – 1898. *Harper's February.*

© Diner Mighty

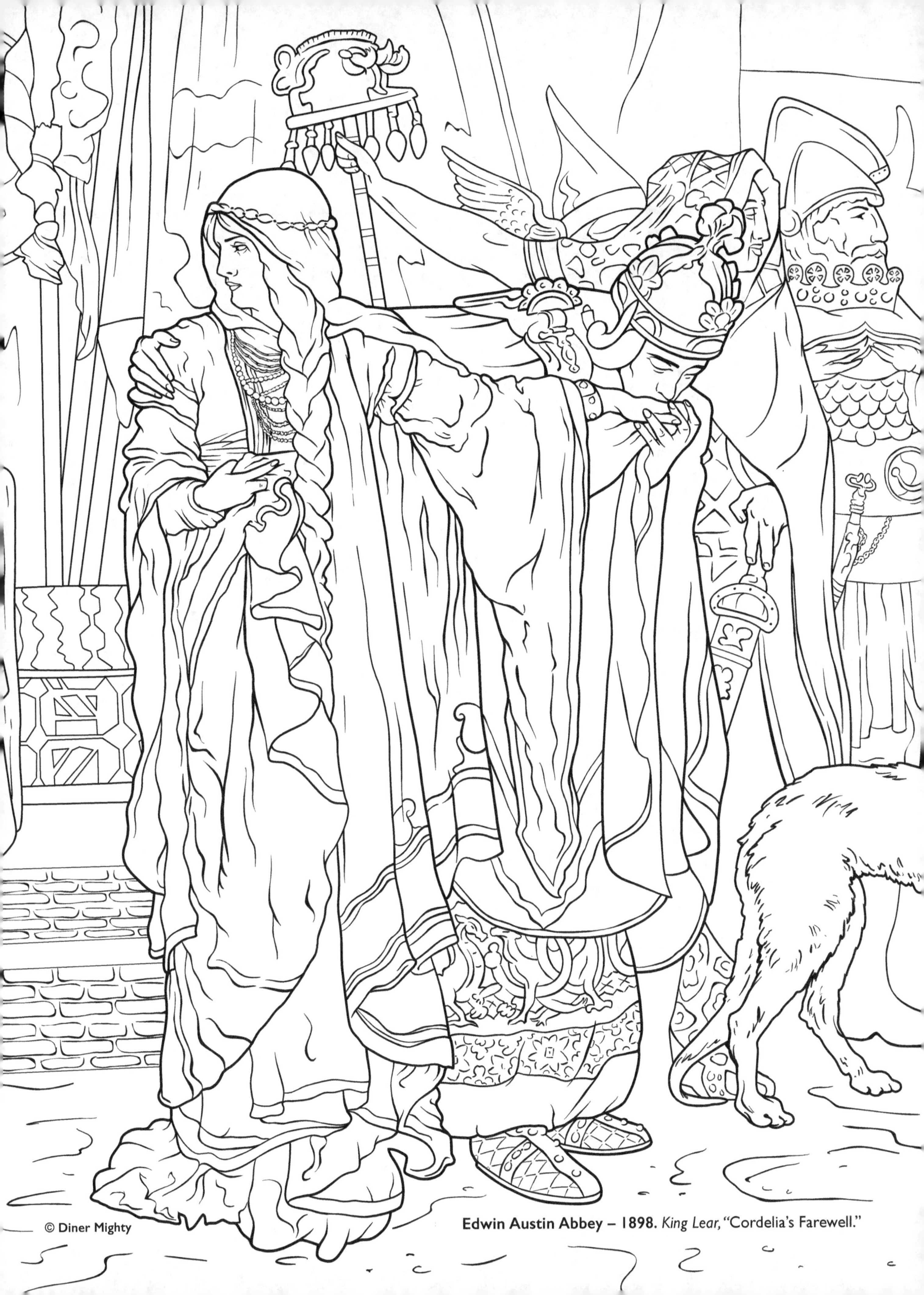

Edwin Austin Abbey – 1898. *King Lear*, "Cordelia's Farewell."

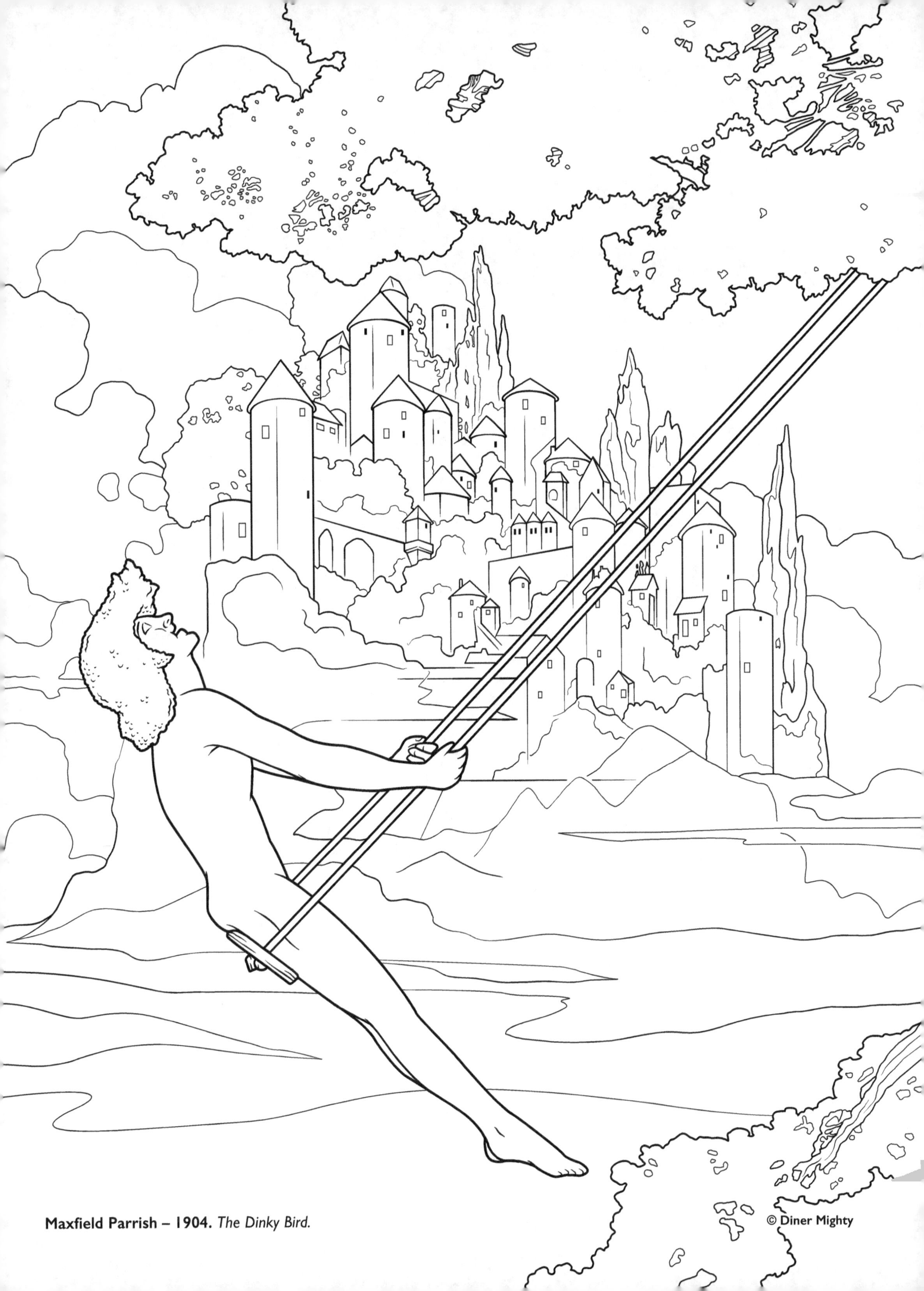

Maxfield Parrish – 1904. *The Dinky Bird.*

© Diner Mighty

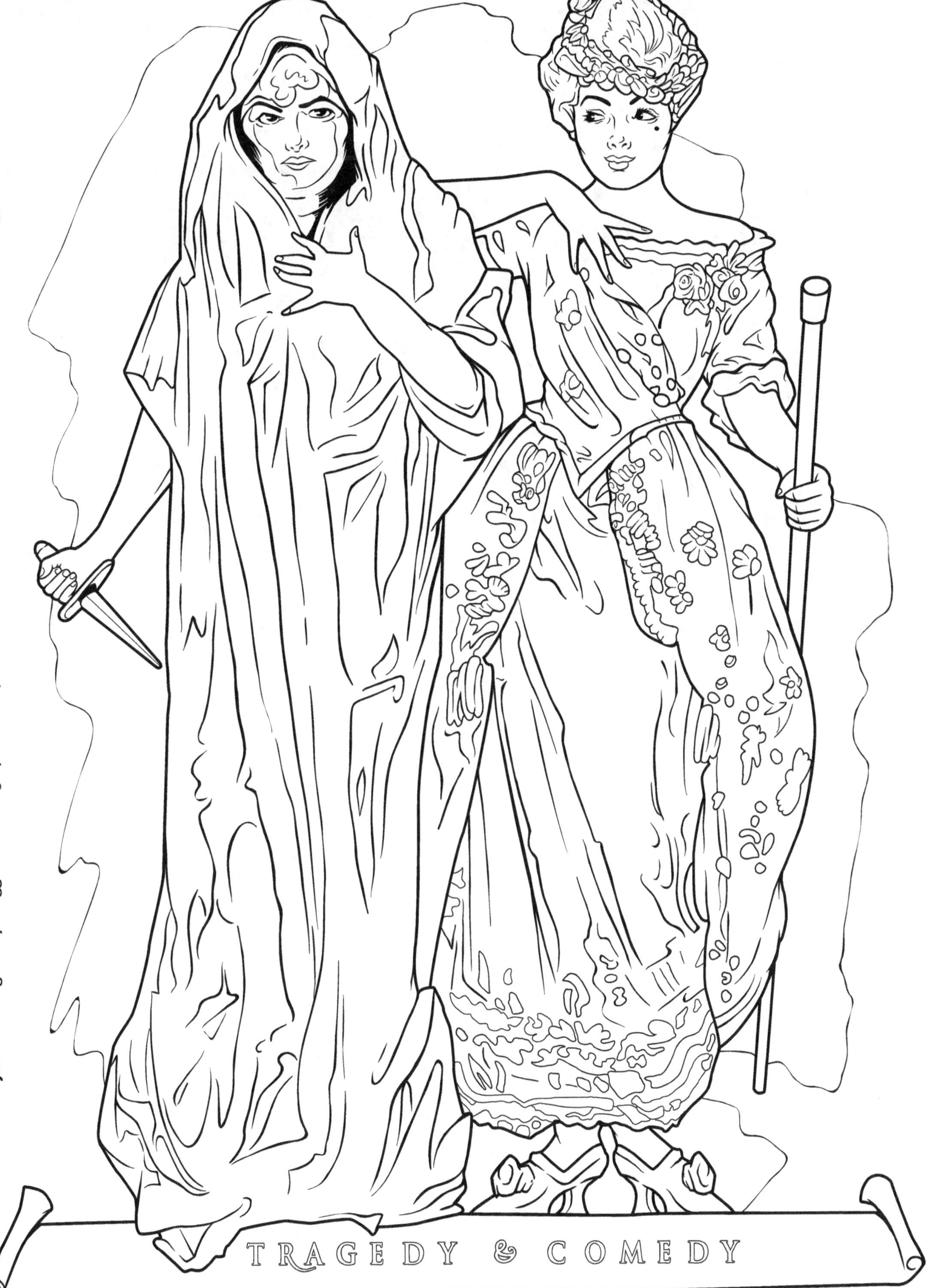

© Diner Mighty
James Montgomery Flagg – 1914. Tragedy & Comedy.
TRAGEDY & COMEDY

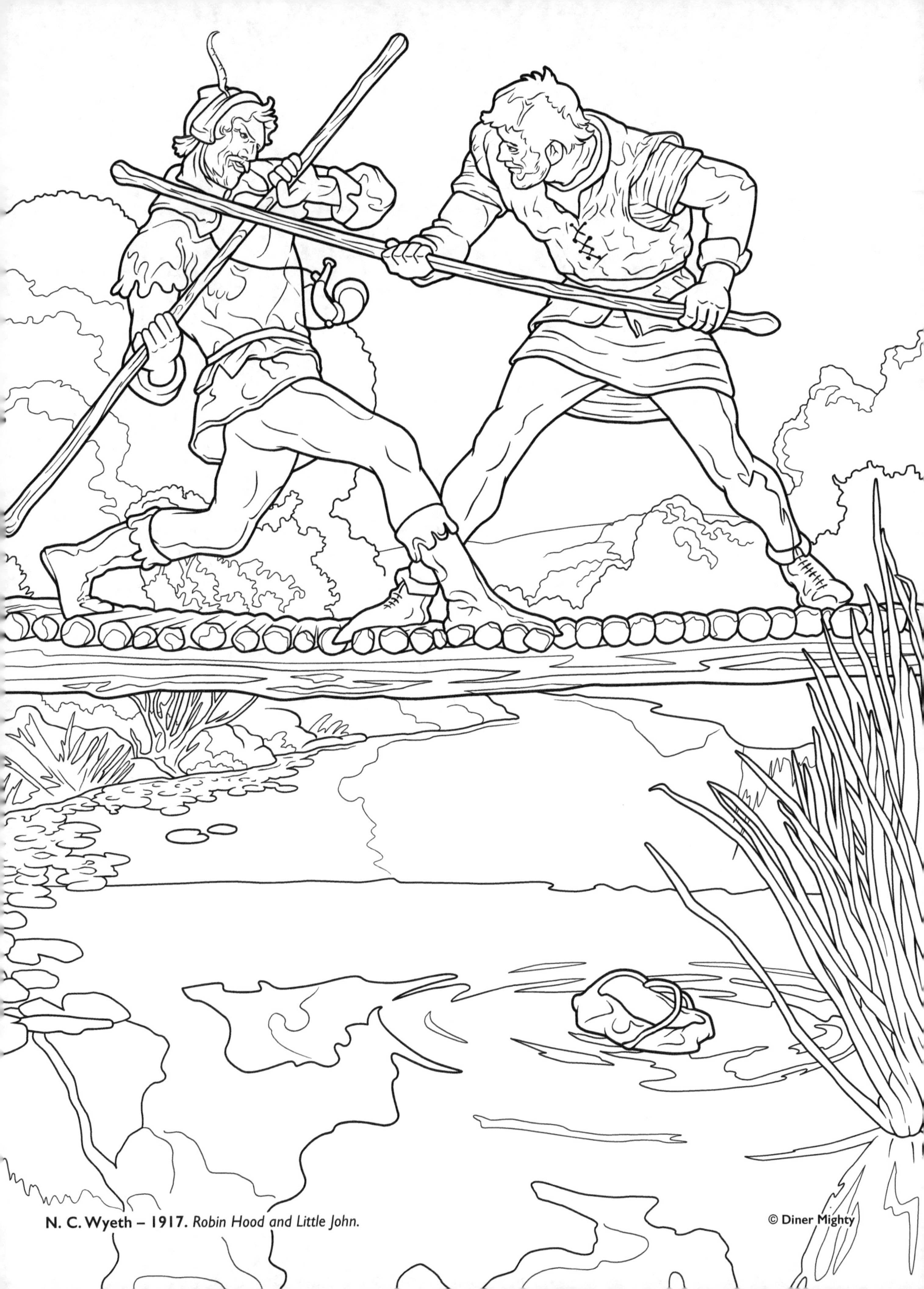

N. C. Wyeth – 1917. *Robin Hood and Little John.*

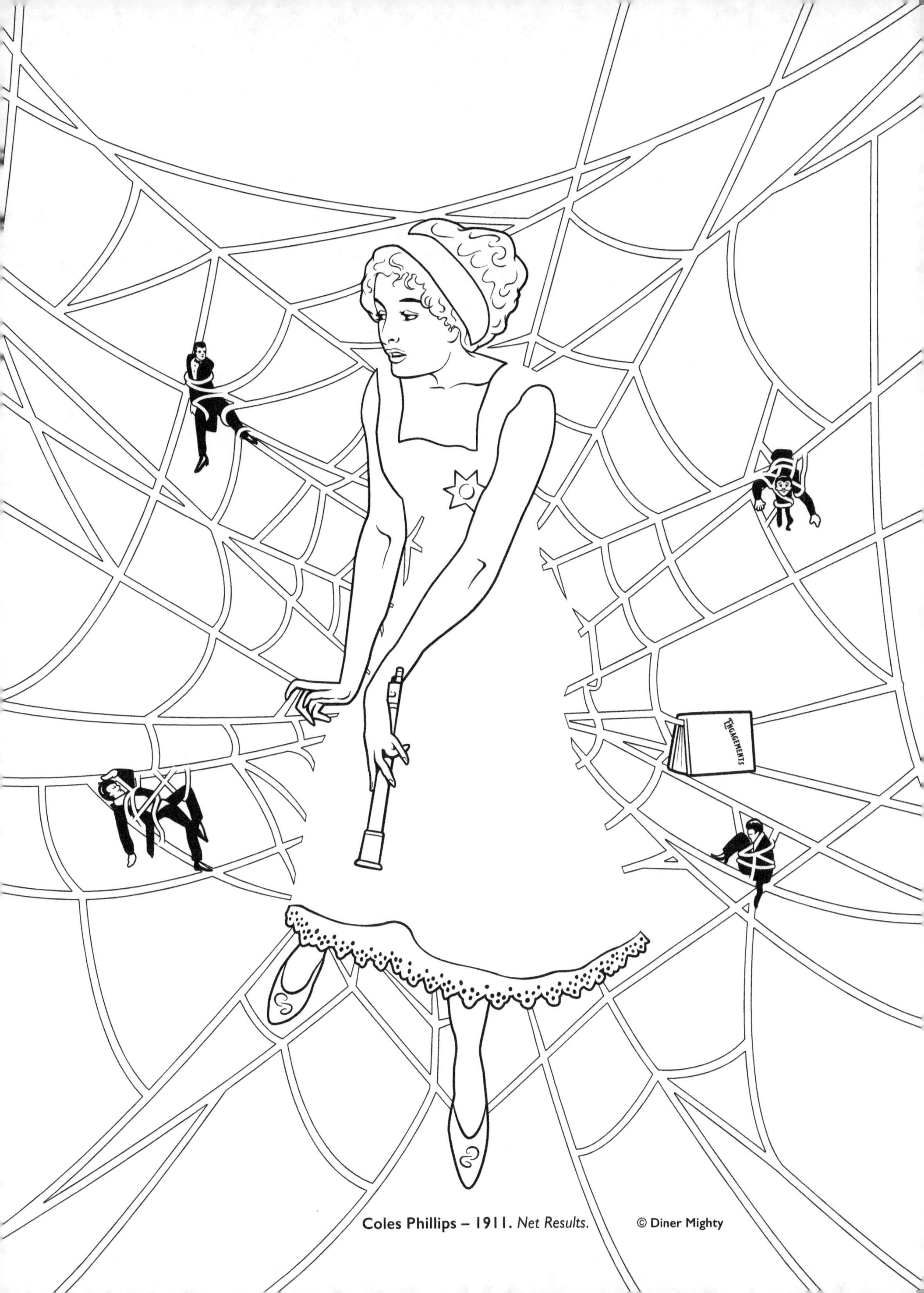

Coles Phillips – 1911. *Net Results.*   © Diner Mighty

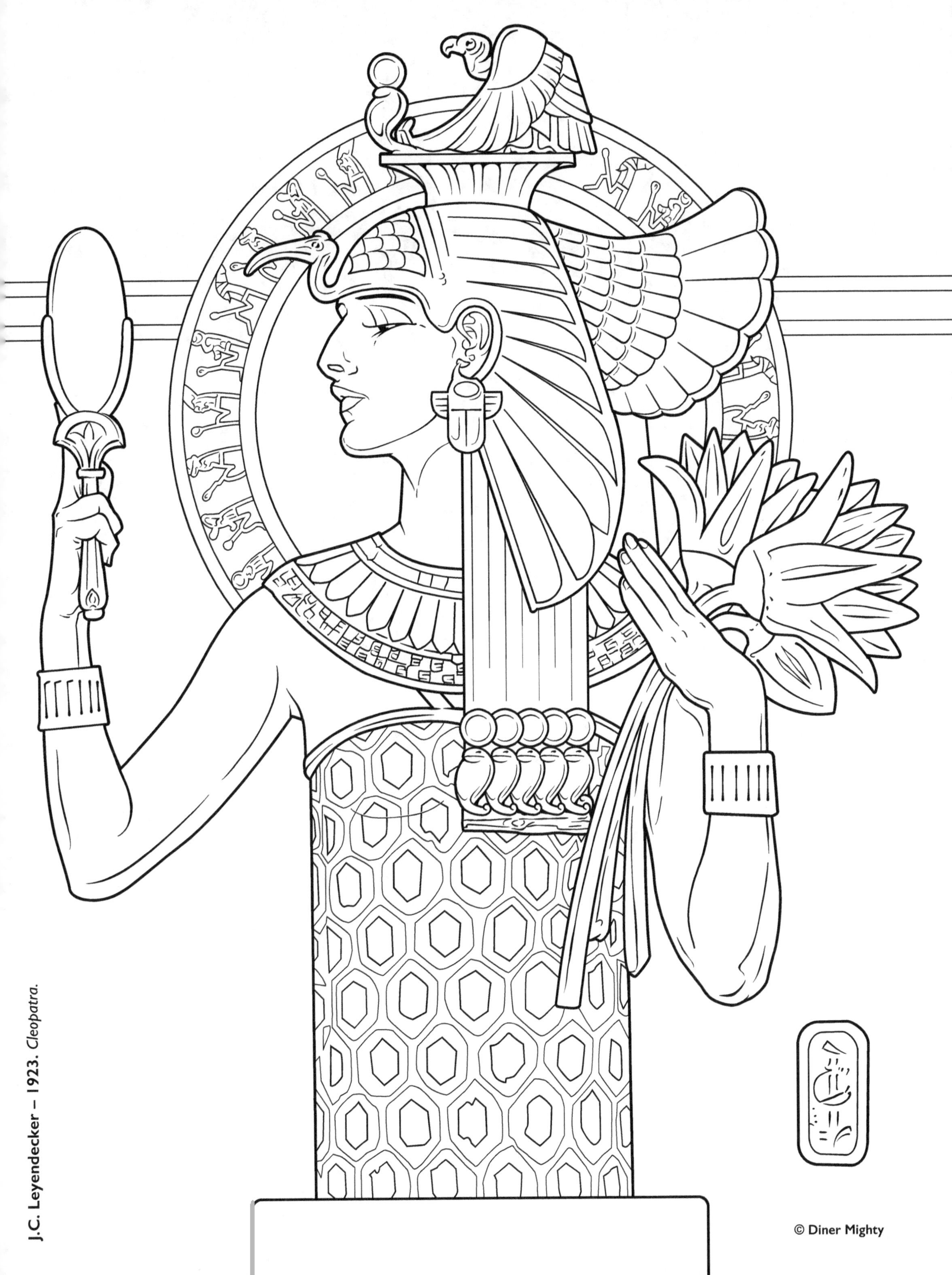

J.C. Leyendecker – 1923. Cleopatra.
© Diner Mighty

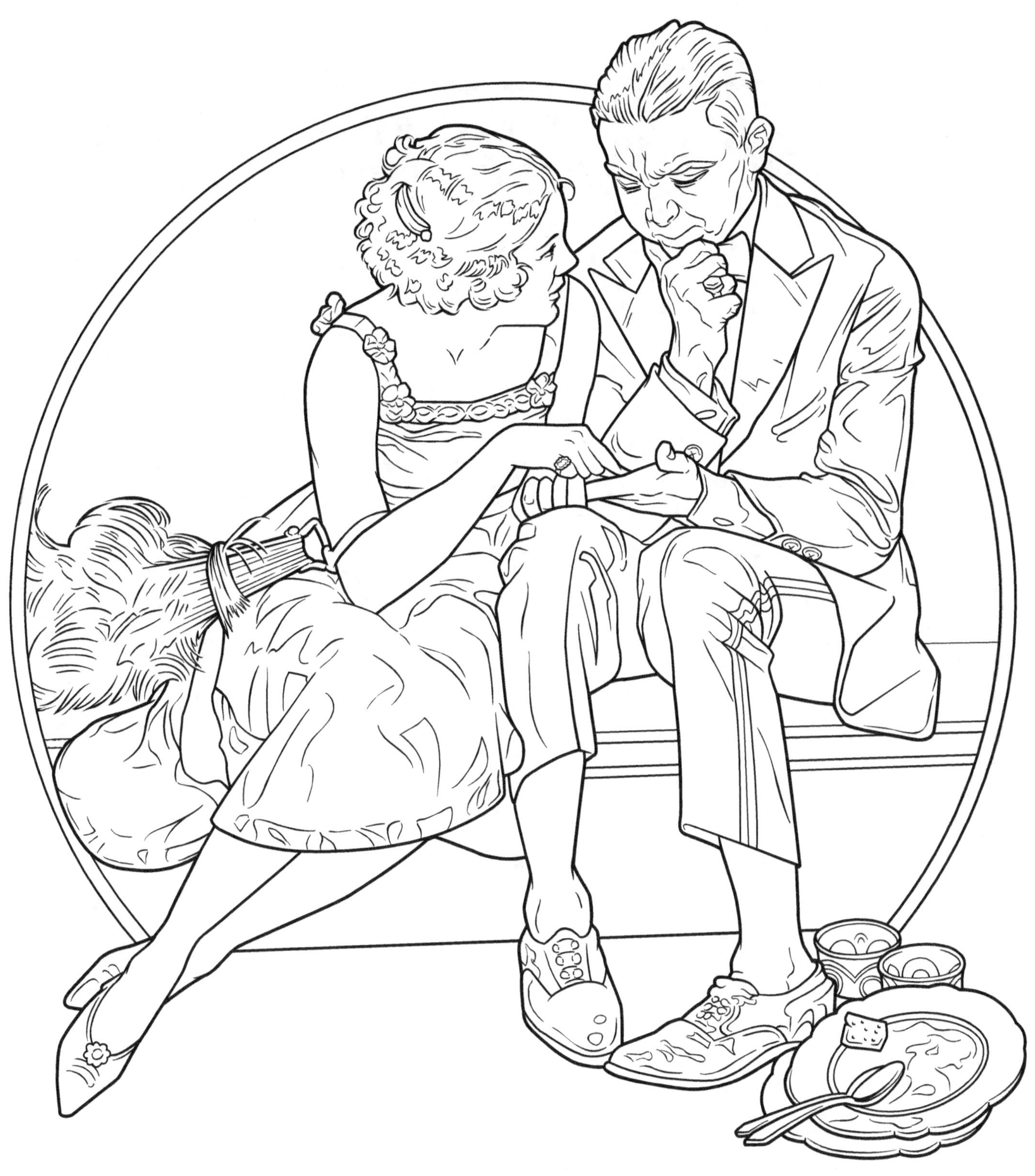

Norman Rockwell – 1921. *Palm reader.*

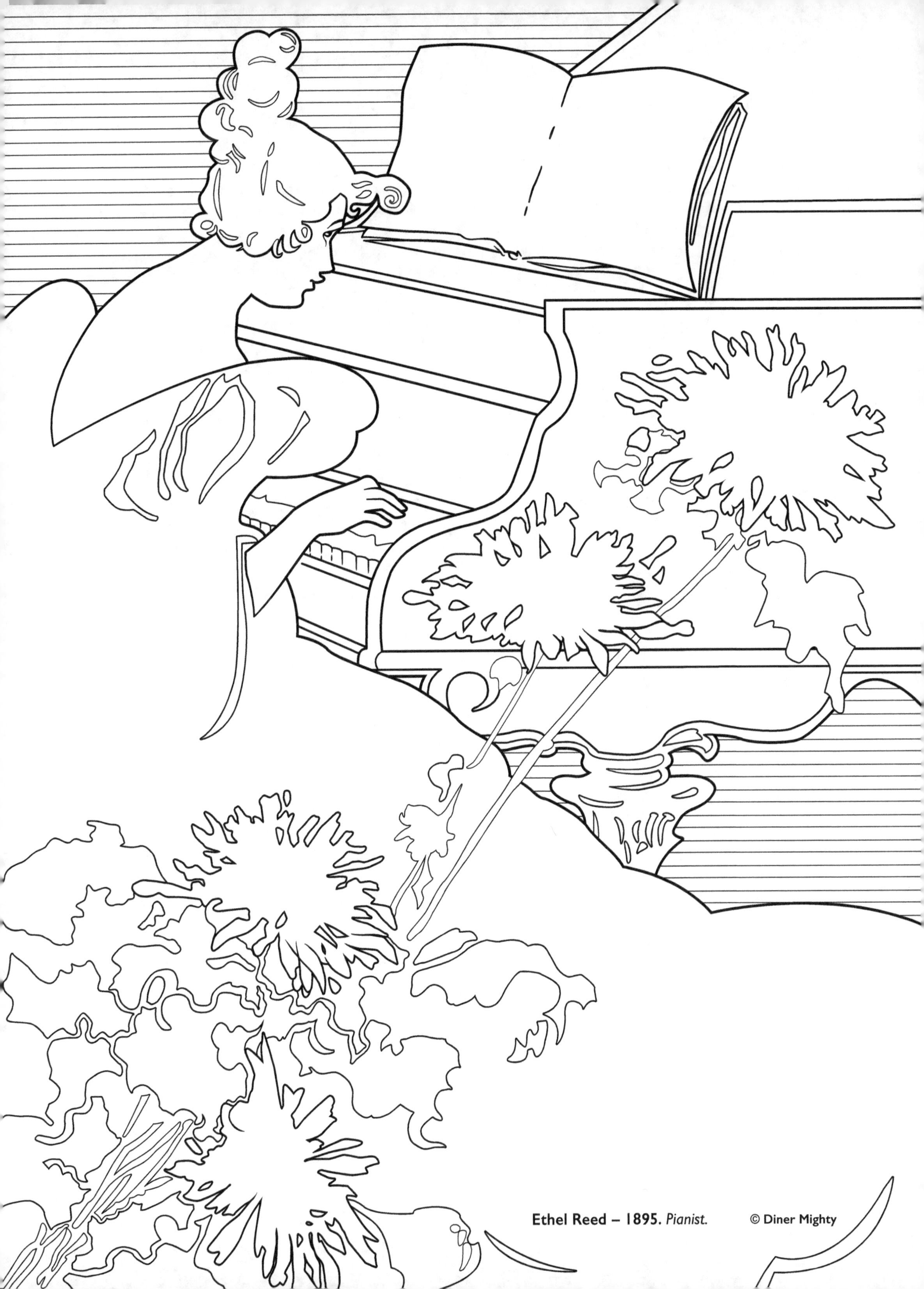

Ethel Reed – 1895. *Pianist.*   © Diner Mighty

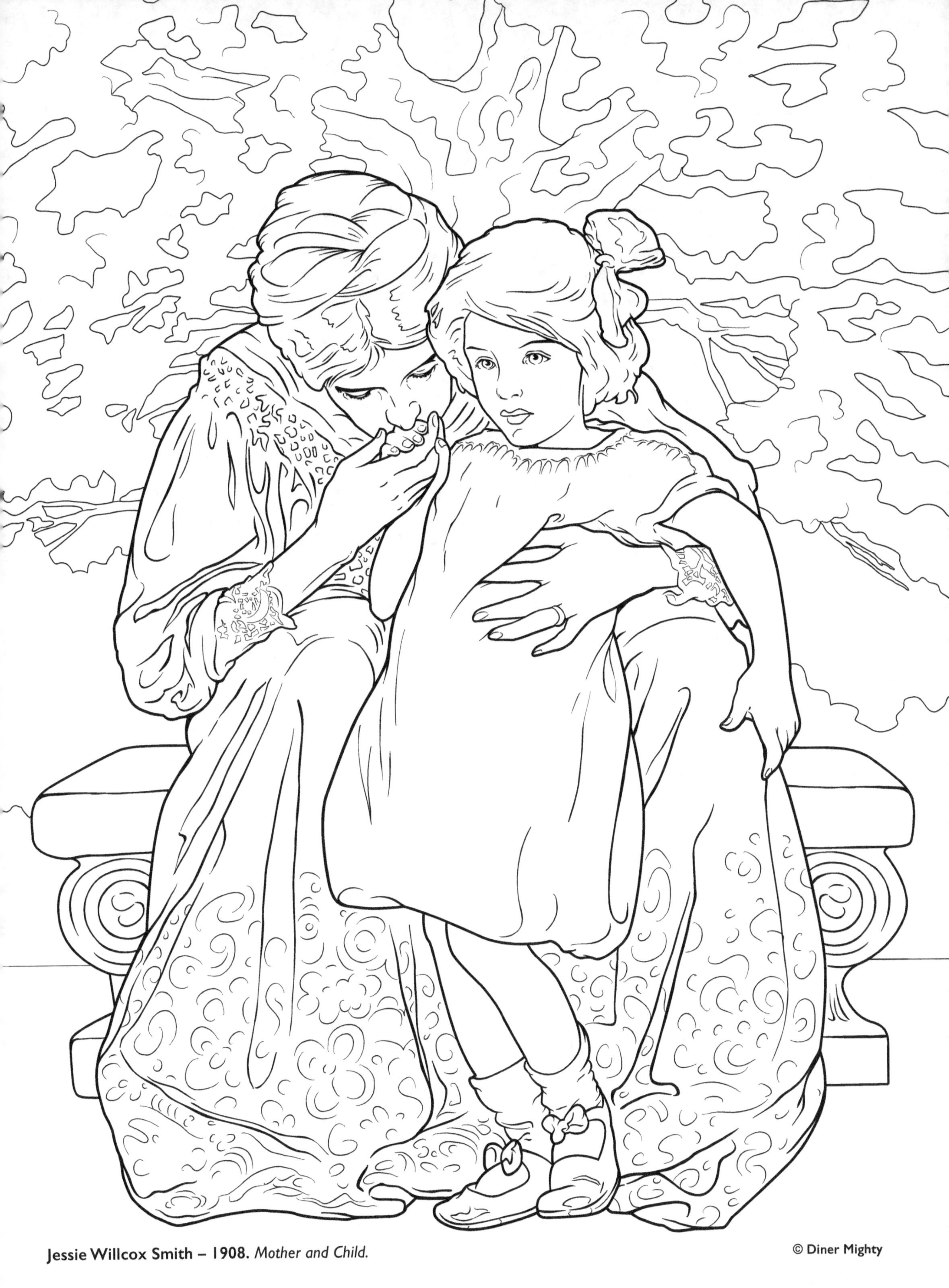

Jessie Willcox Smith – 1908. *Mother and Child.*

© Diner Mighty

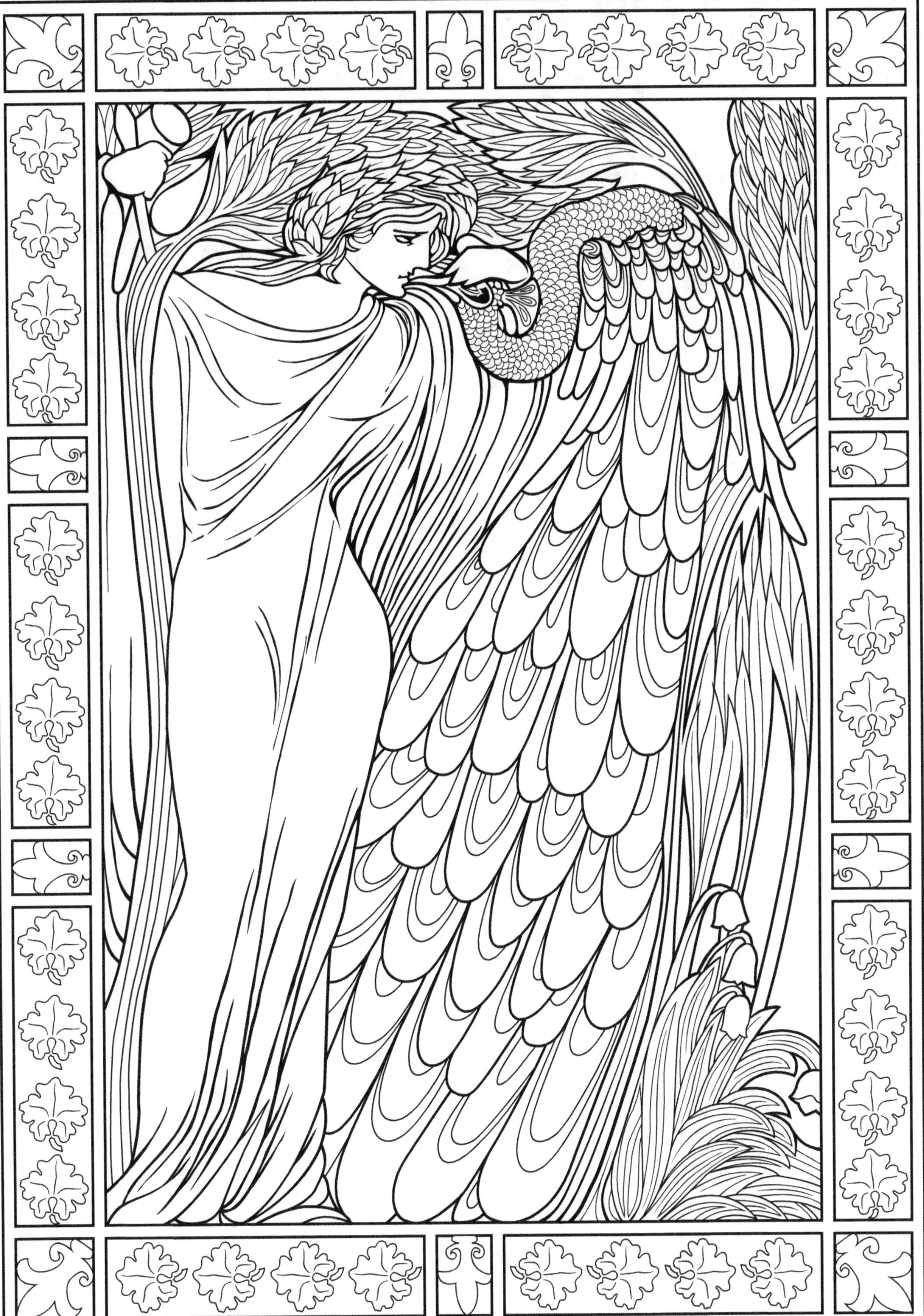
© Diner Mighty
Will H. Bradley – 1896. Woman with peacock.

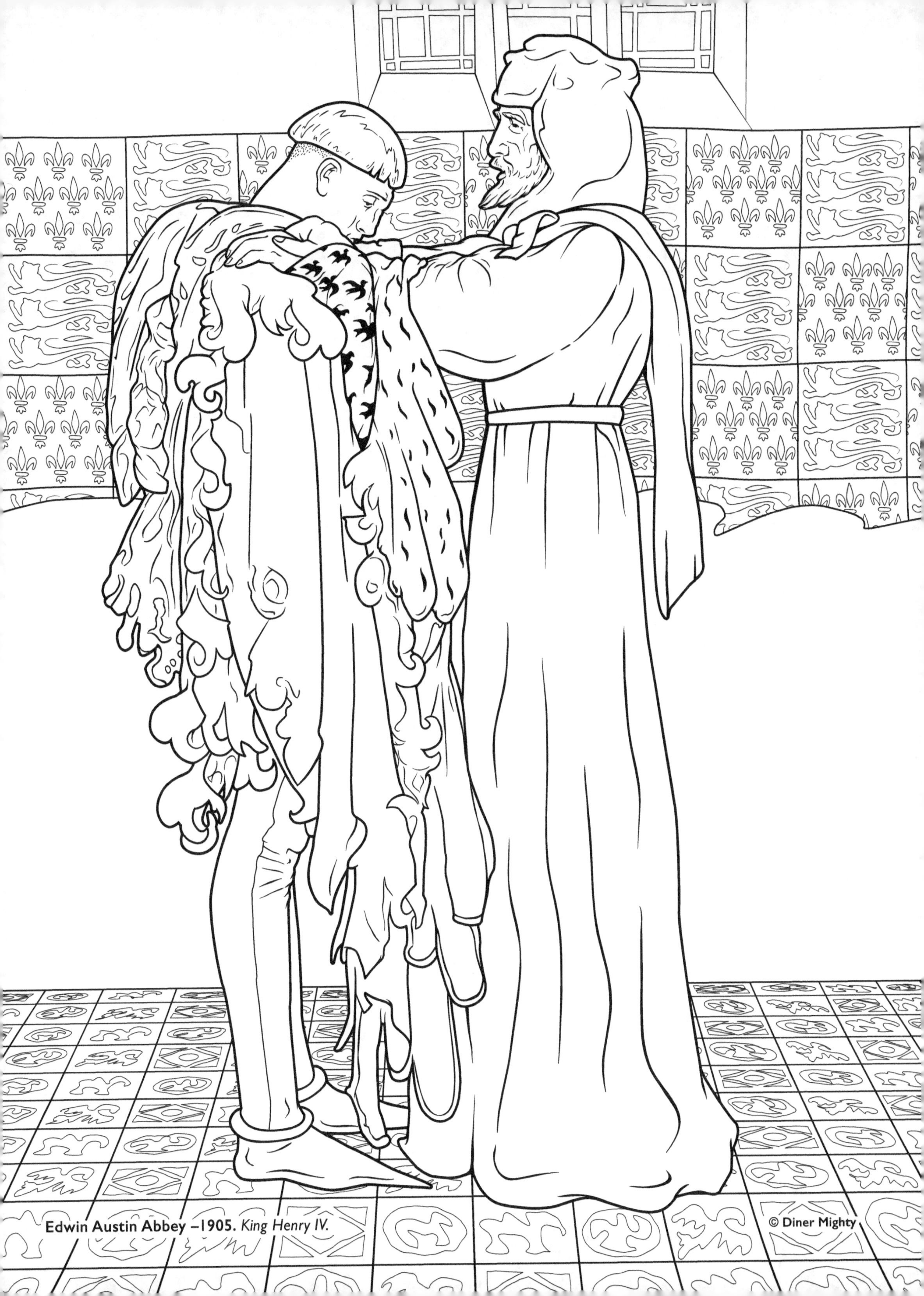

Edwin Austin Abbey –1905. King Henry IV.
© Diner Mighty

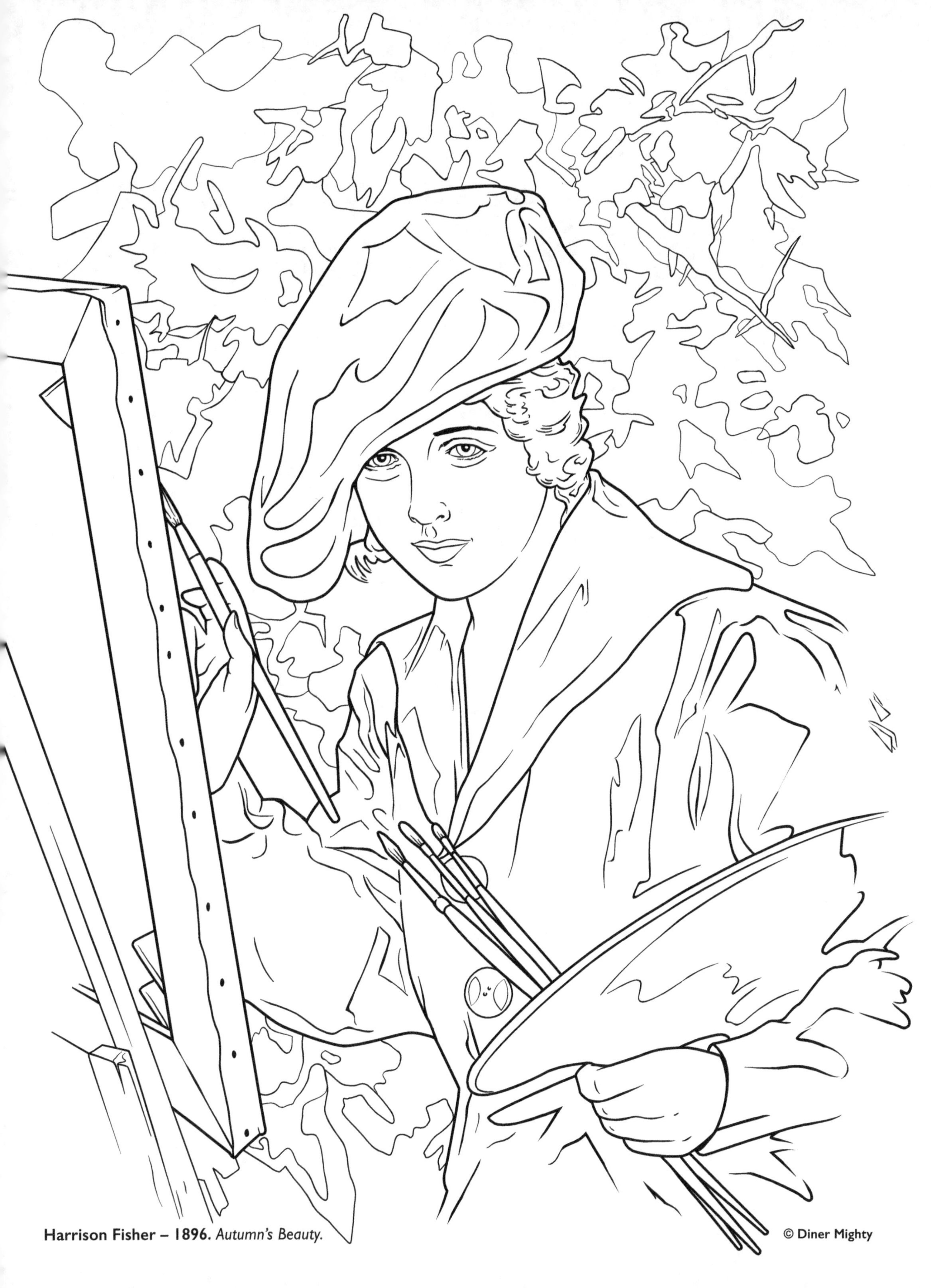

Harrison Fisher – 1896. *Autumn's Beauty.*

© Diner Mighty

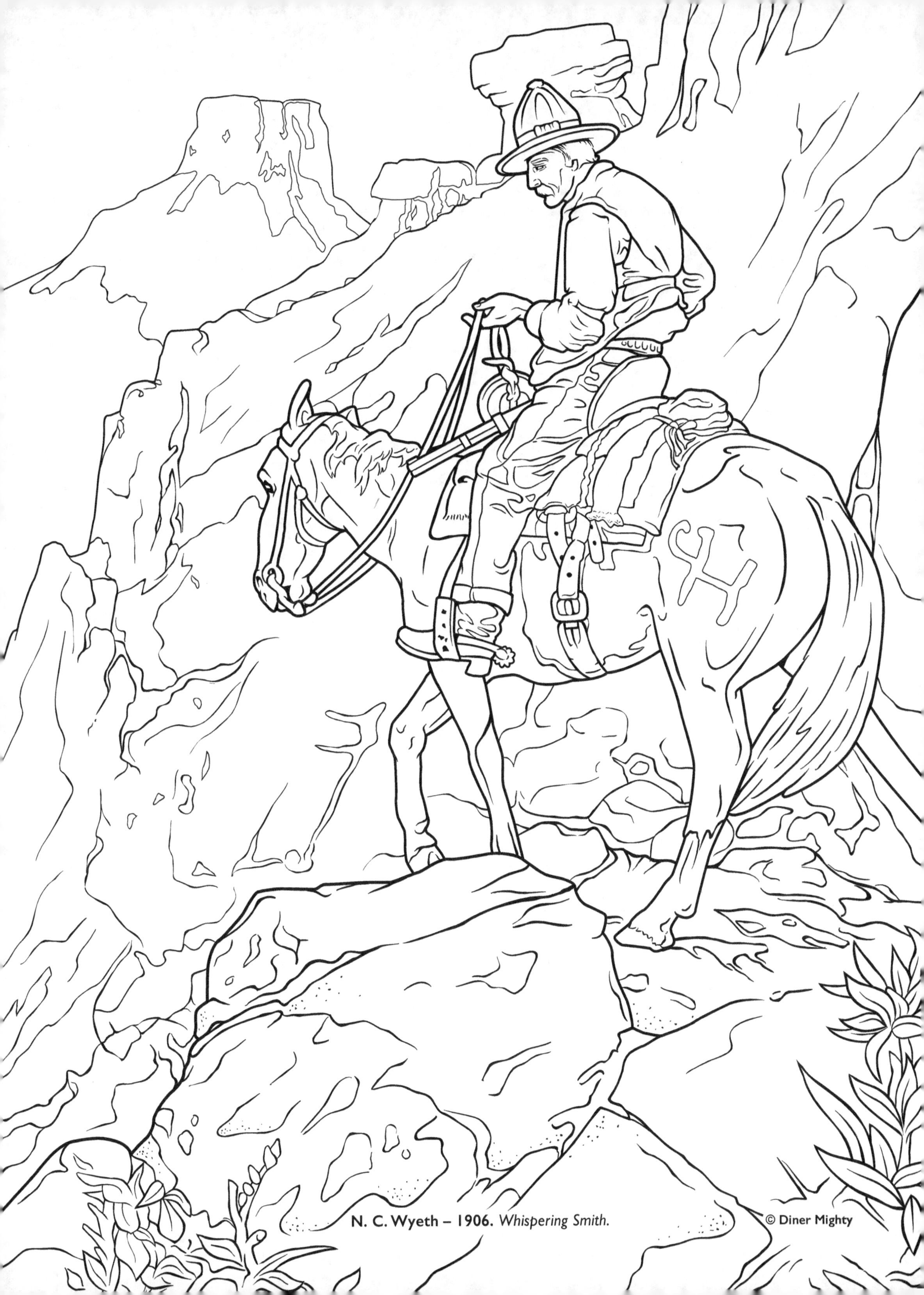

N. C. Wyeth – 1906. Whispering Smith.

© Diner Mighty

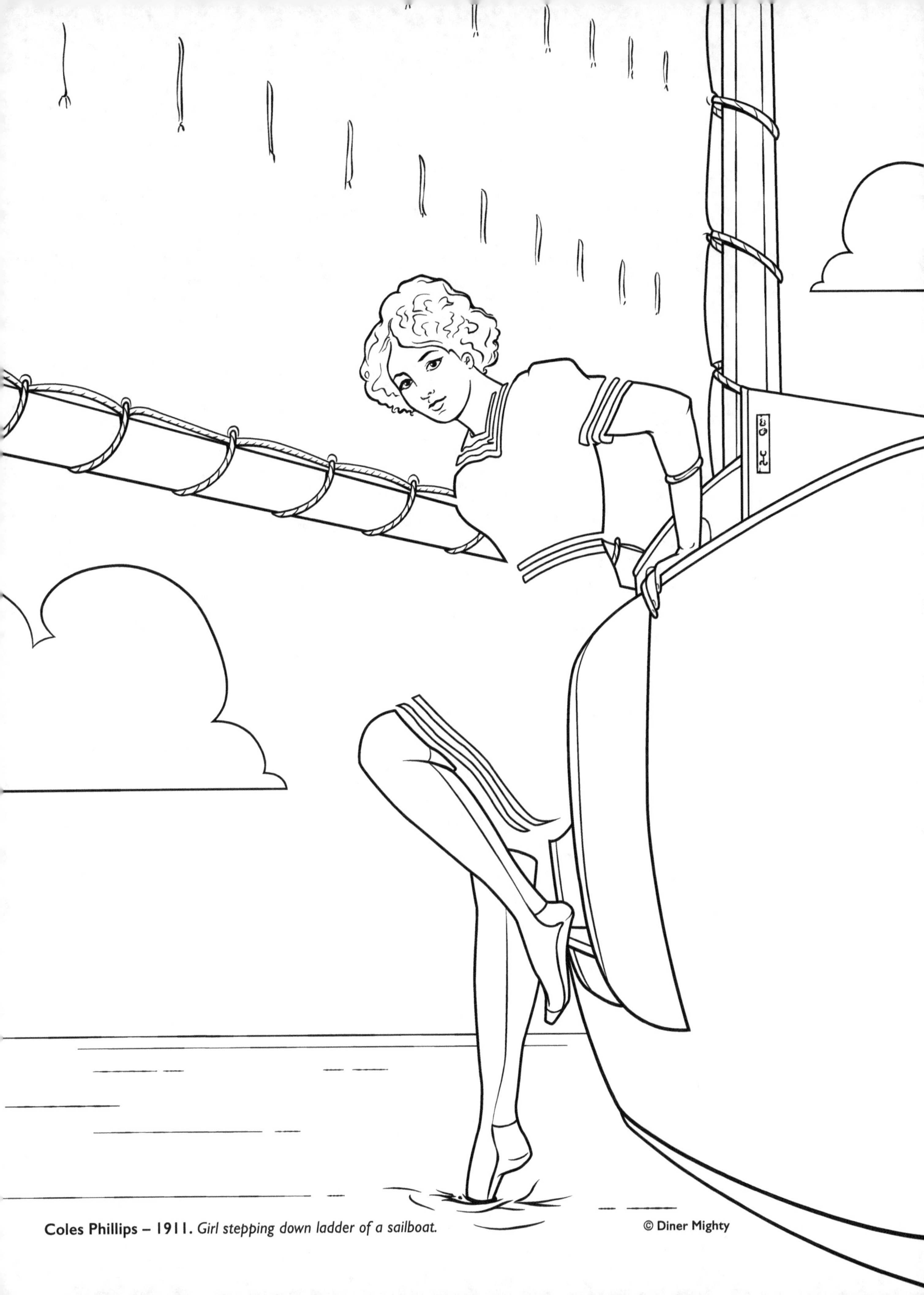

Coles Phillips – 1911. *Girl stepping down ladder of a sailboat.*

© Diner Mighty

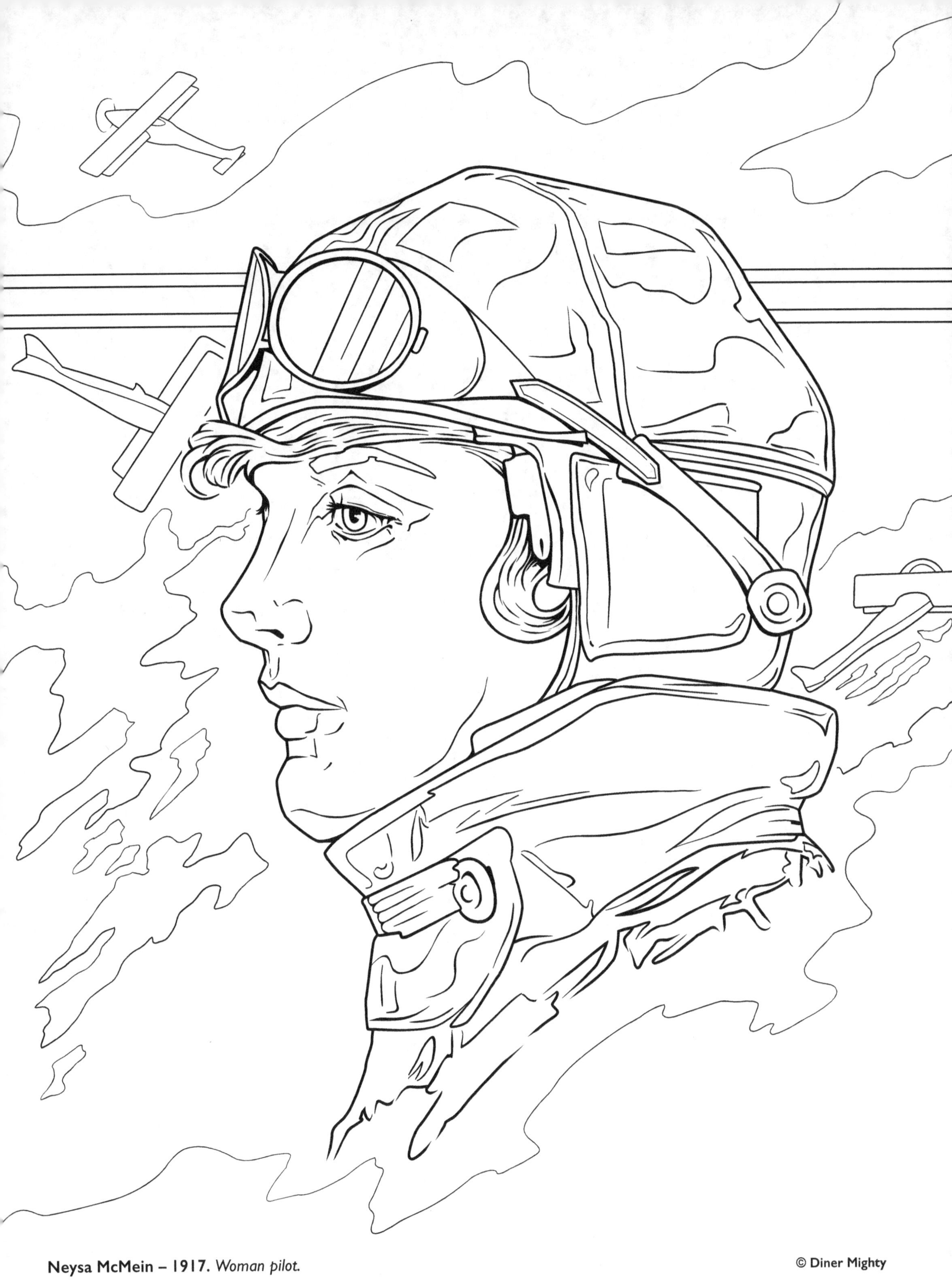

Neysa McMein – 1917. *Woman pilot.*

© Diner Mighty

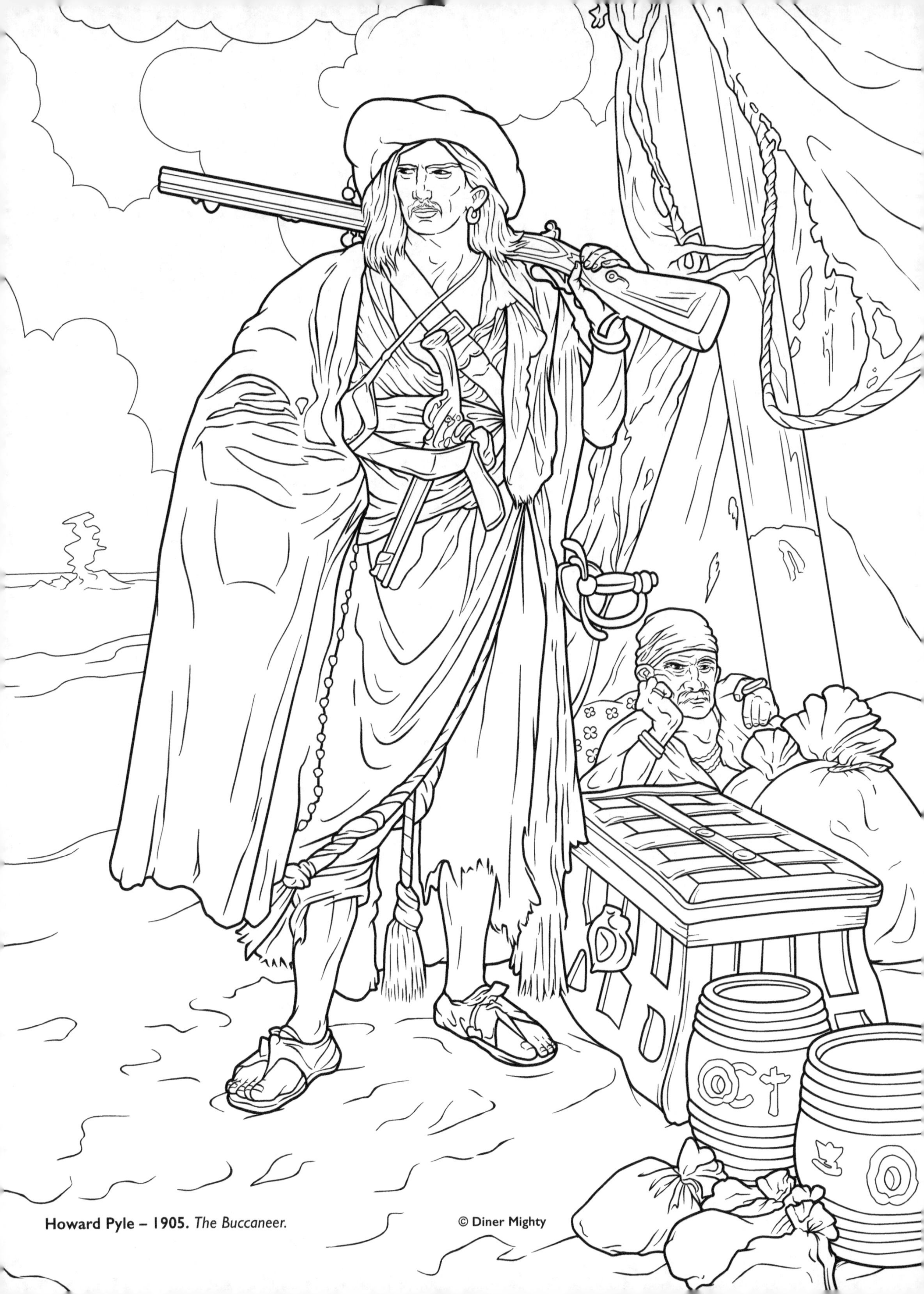

Howard Pyle – 1905. *The Buccaneer.*   © Diner Mighty

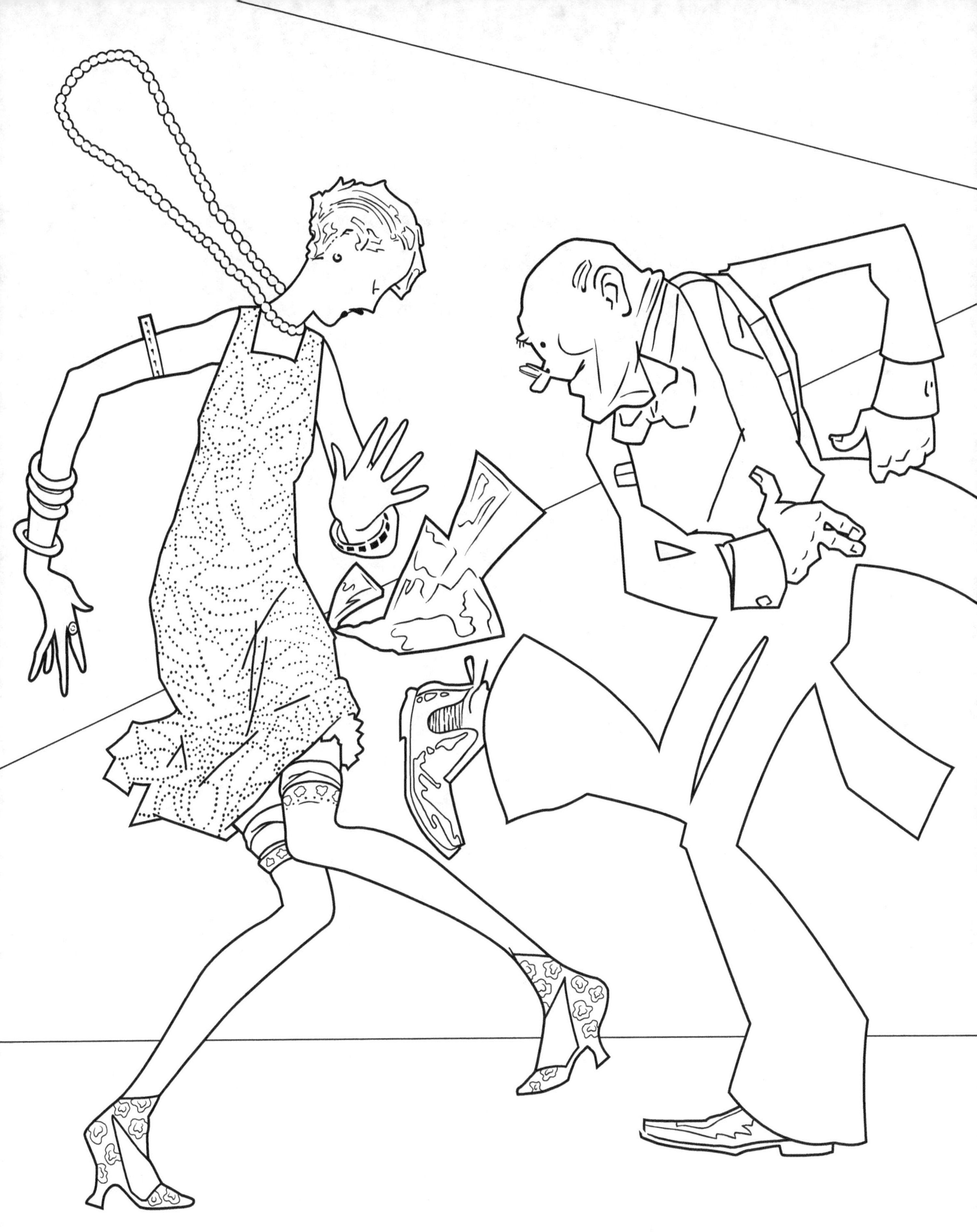

John Held Jr. – 1926. *Jazz dancers.*

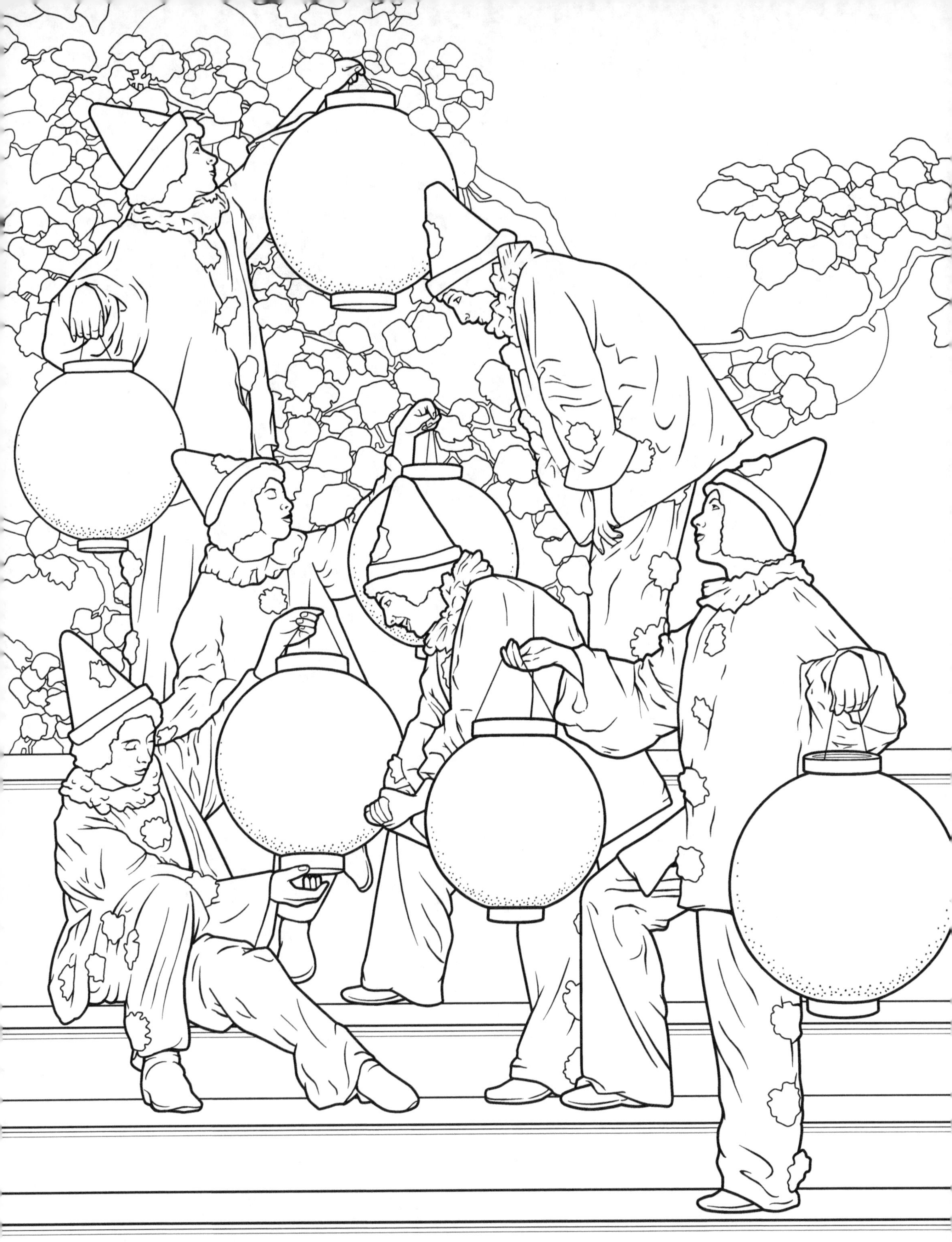

Maxfield Parrish – 1910. *The Lantern Bearers.*

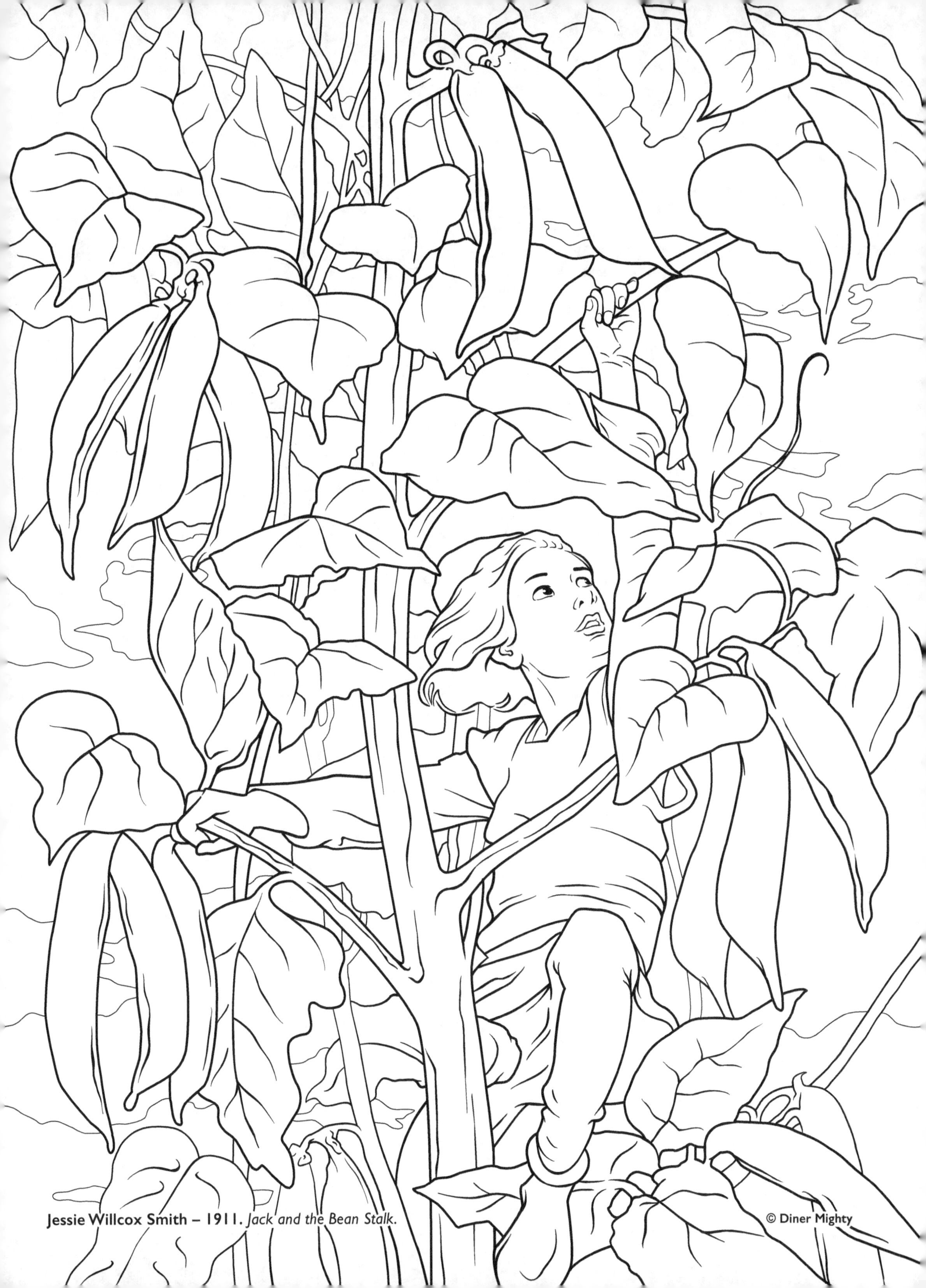

Jessie Willcox Smith – 1911. *Jack and the Bean Stalk.*

© Diner Mighty

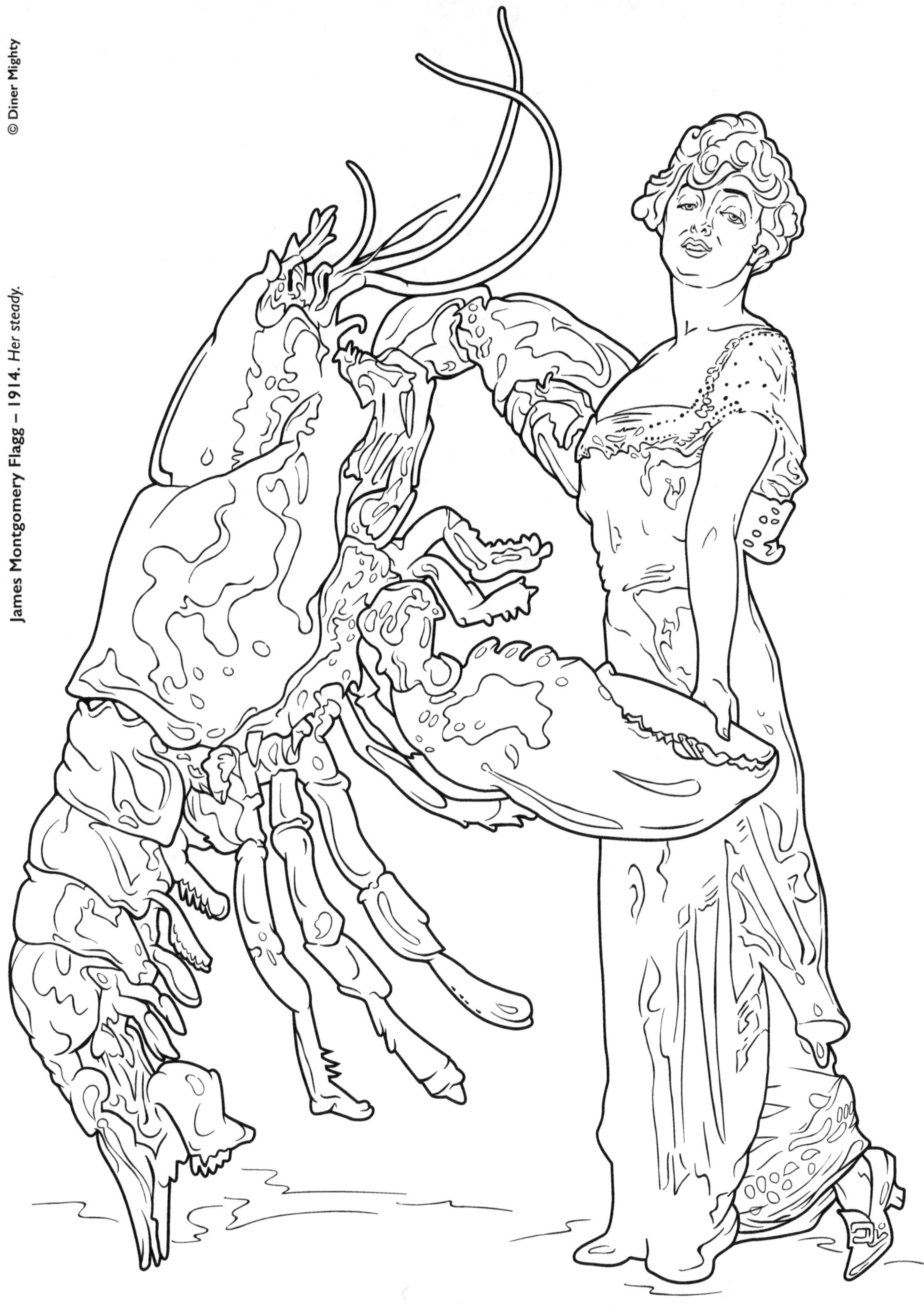

James Montgomery Flagg – 1914. *Her steady.*

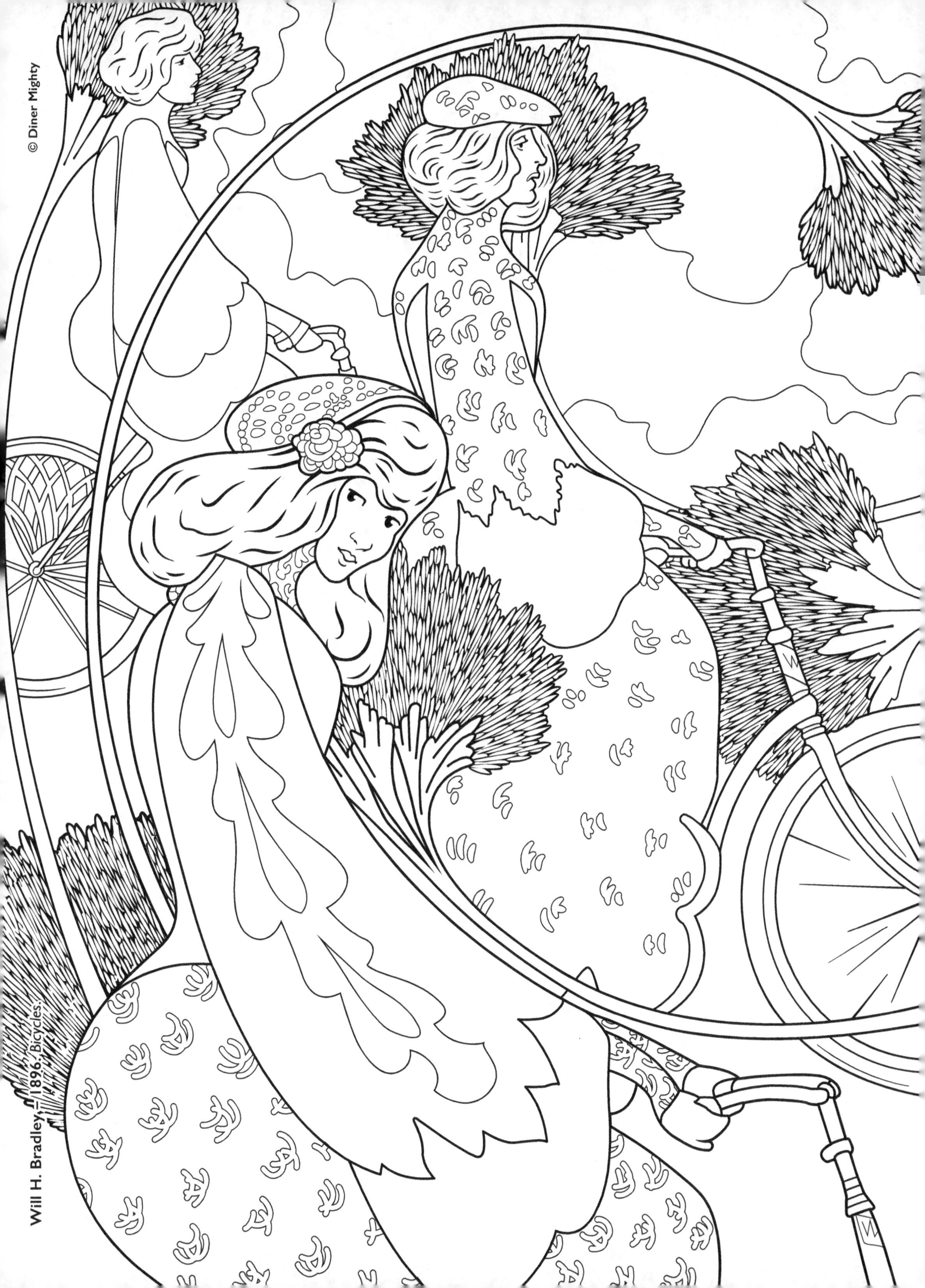

© Diner Mighty
Will H. Bradley, 1896. Bicycles.

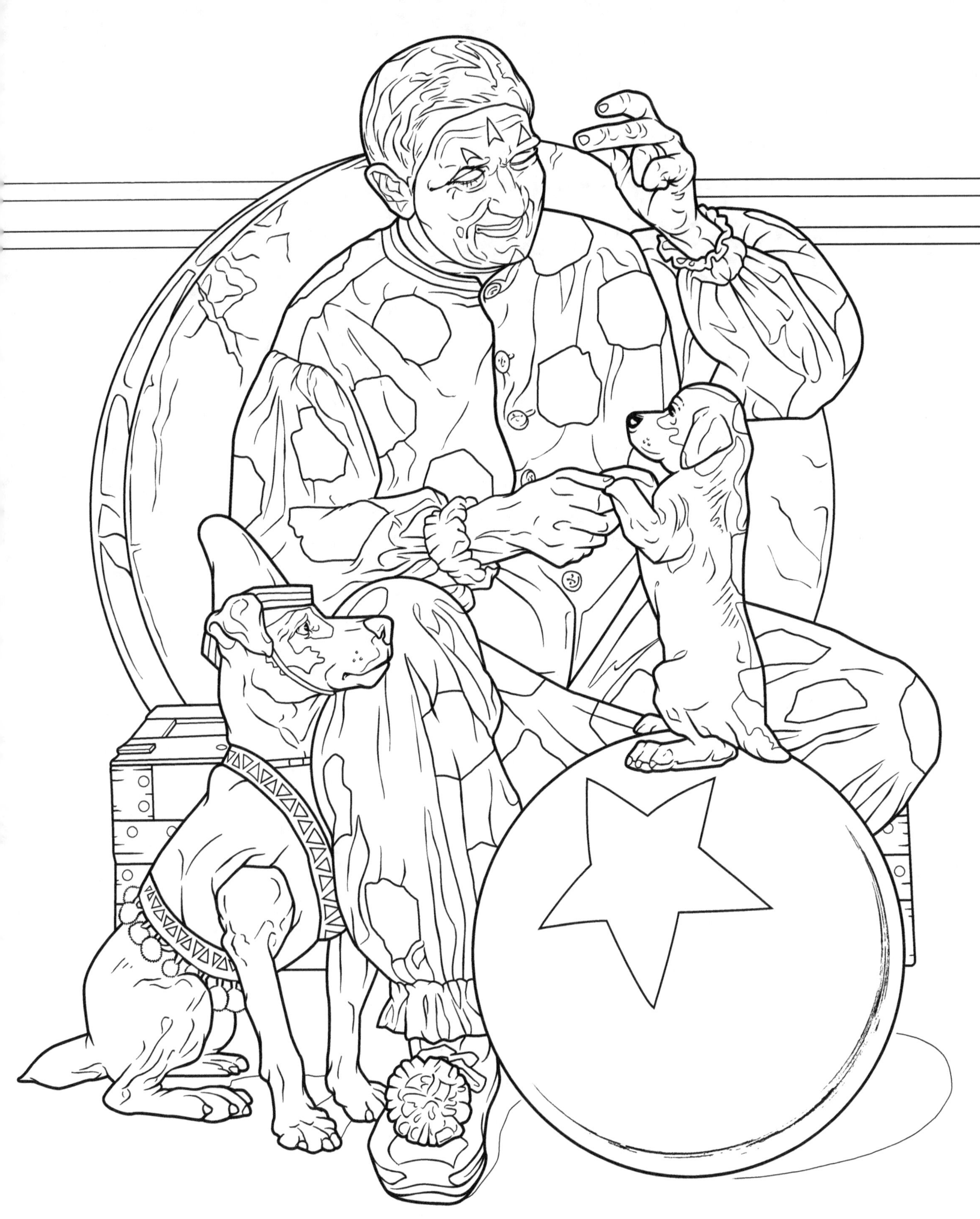

Norman Rockwell – 1923. *Circus clown and dogs.*

© Diner Mighty

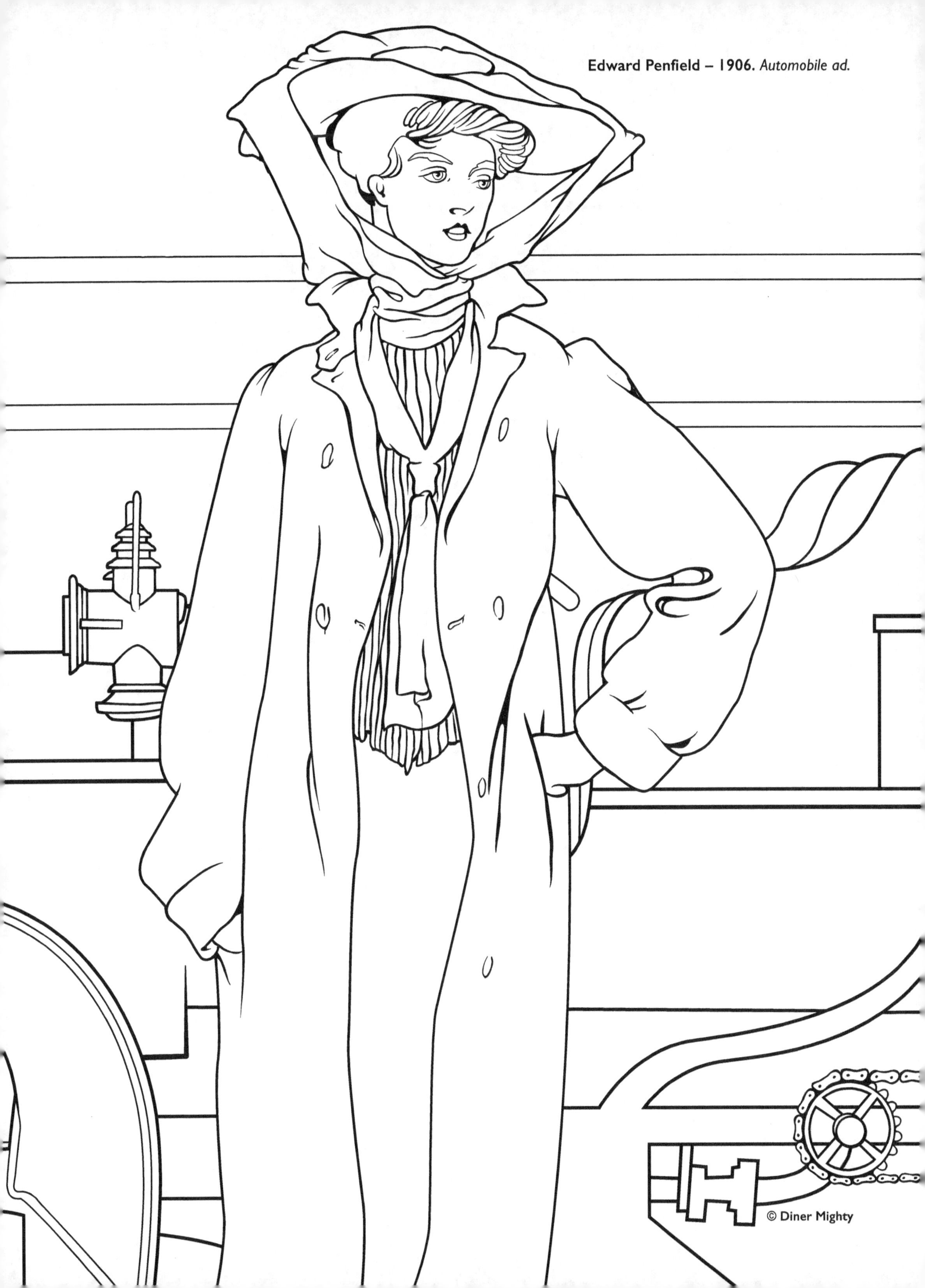

Edward Penfield – 1906. Automobile ad.
© Diner Mighty

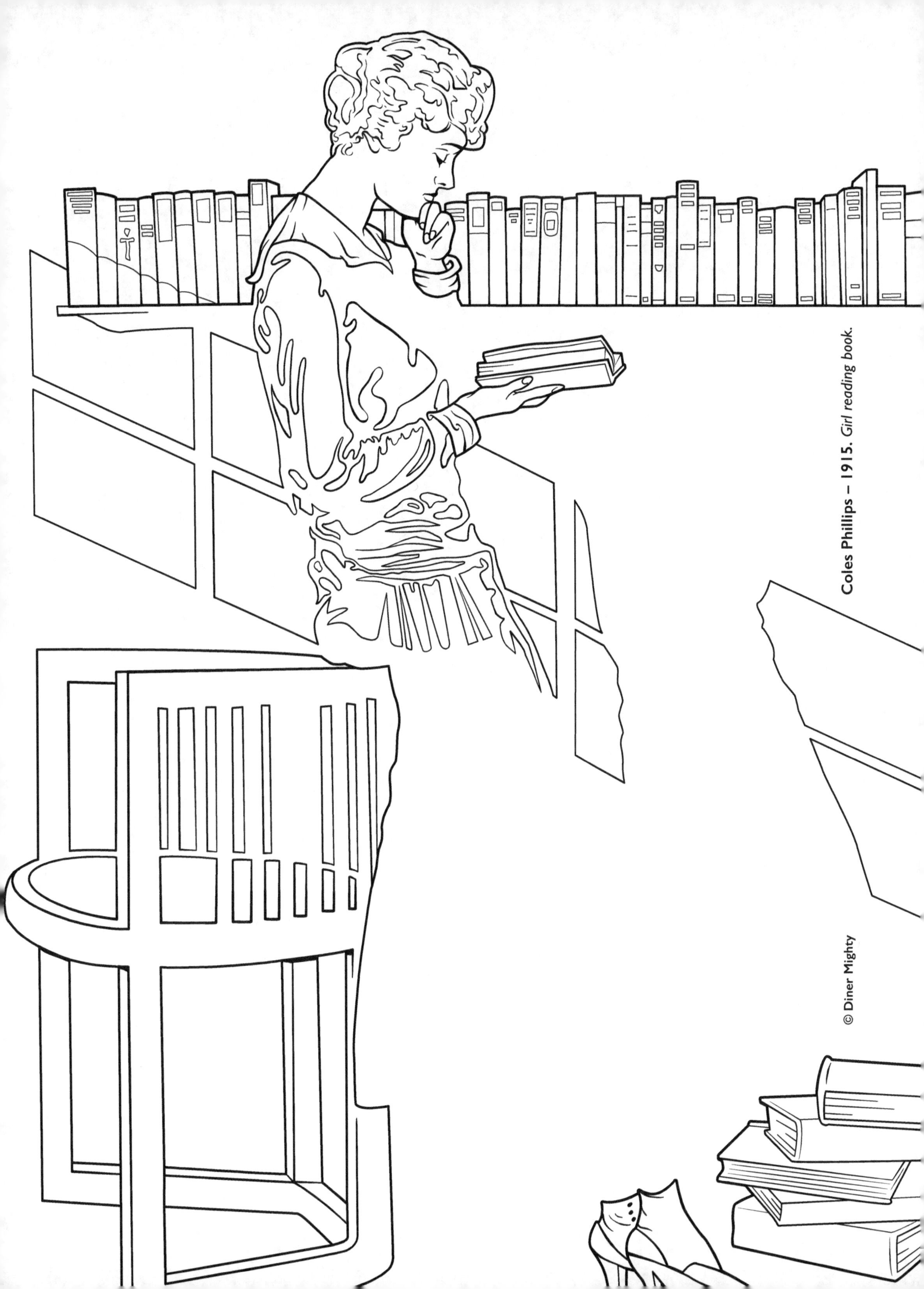

Coles Phillips – 1915. *Girl reading book.*
© Diner Mighty

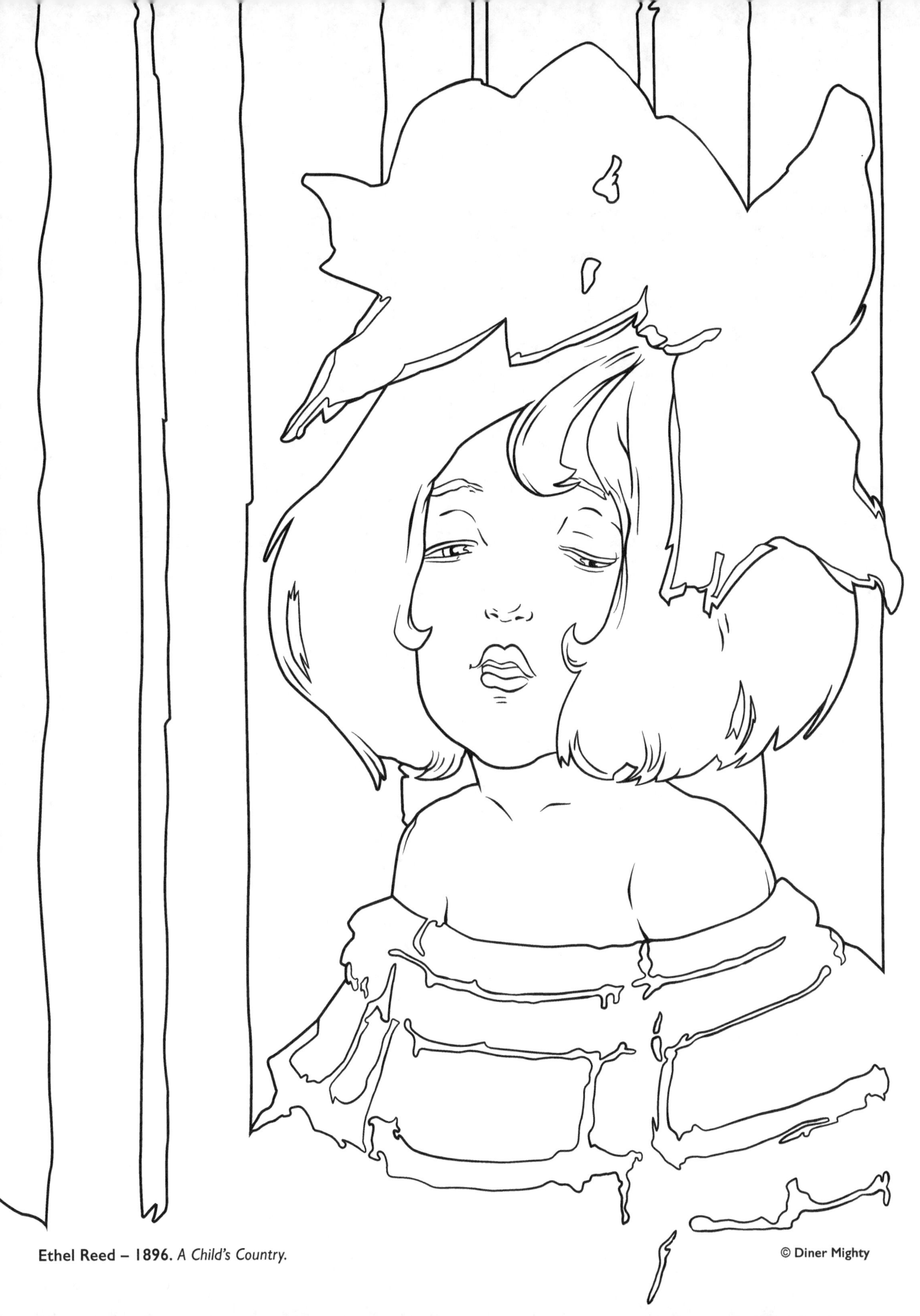

Ethel Reed – 1896. *A Child's Country.*

© Diner Mighty

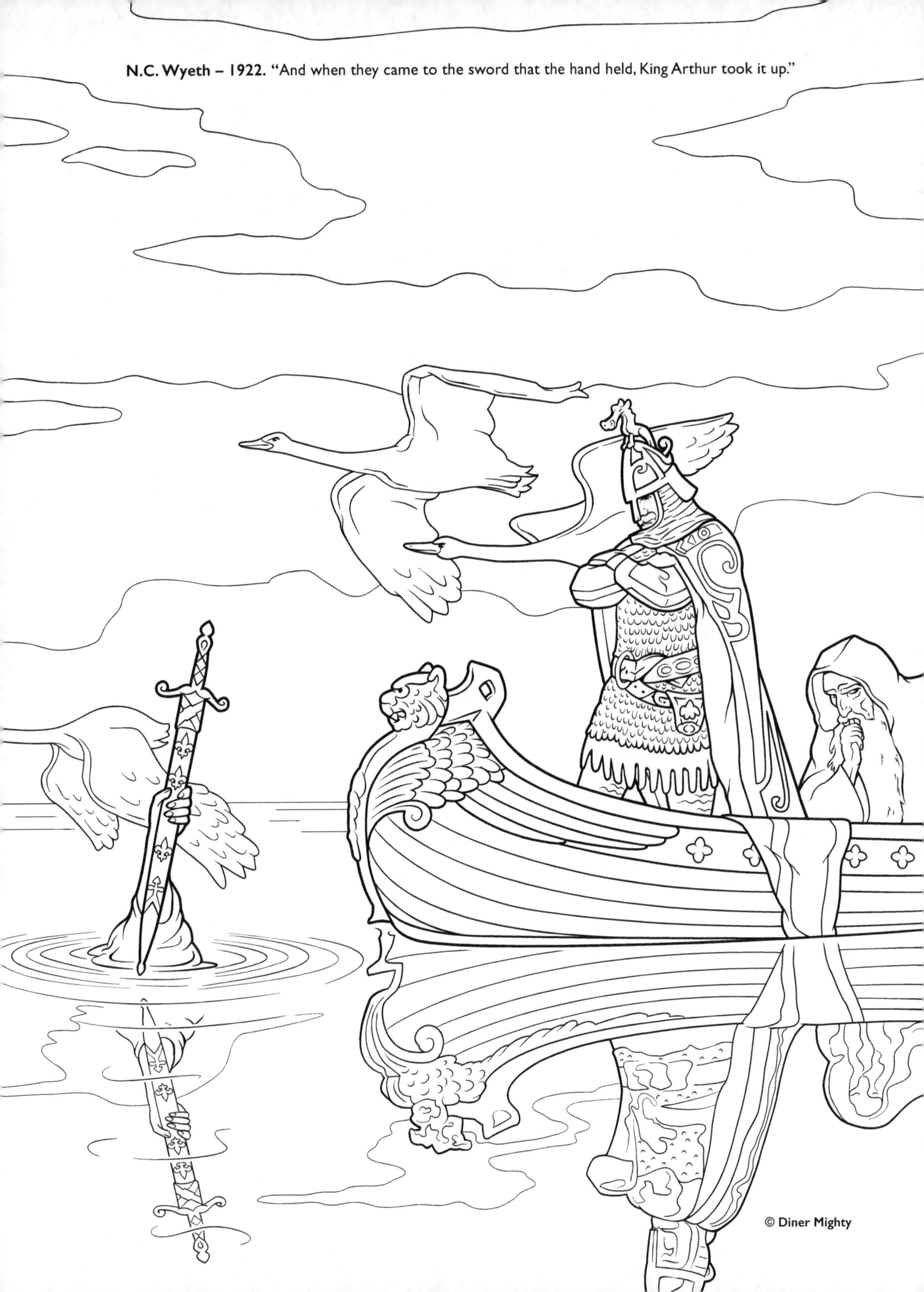

N.C. Wyeth – 1922. "And when they came to the sword that the hand held, King Arthur took it up."
© Diner Mighty

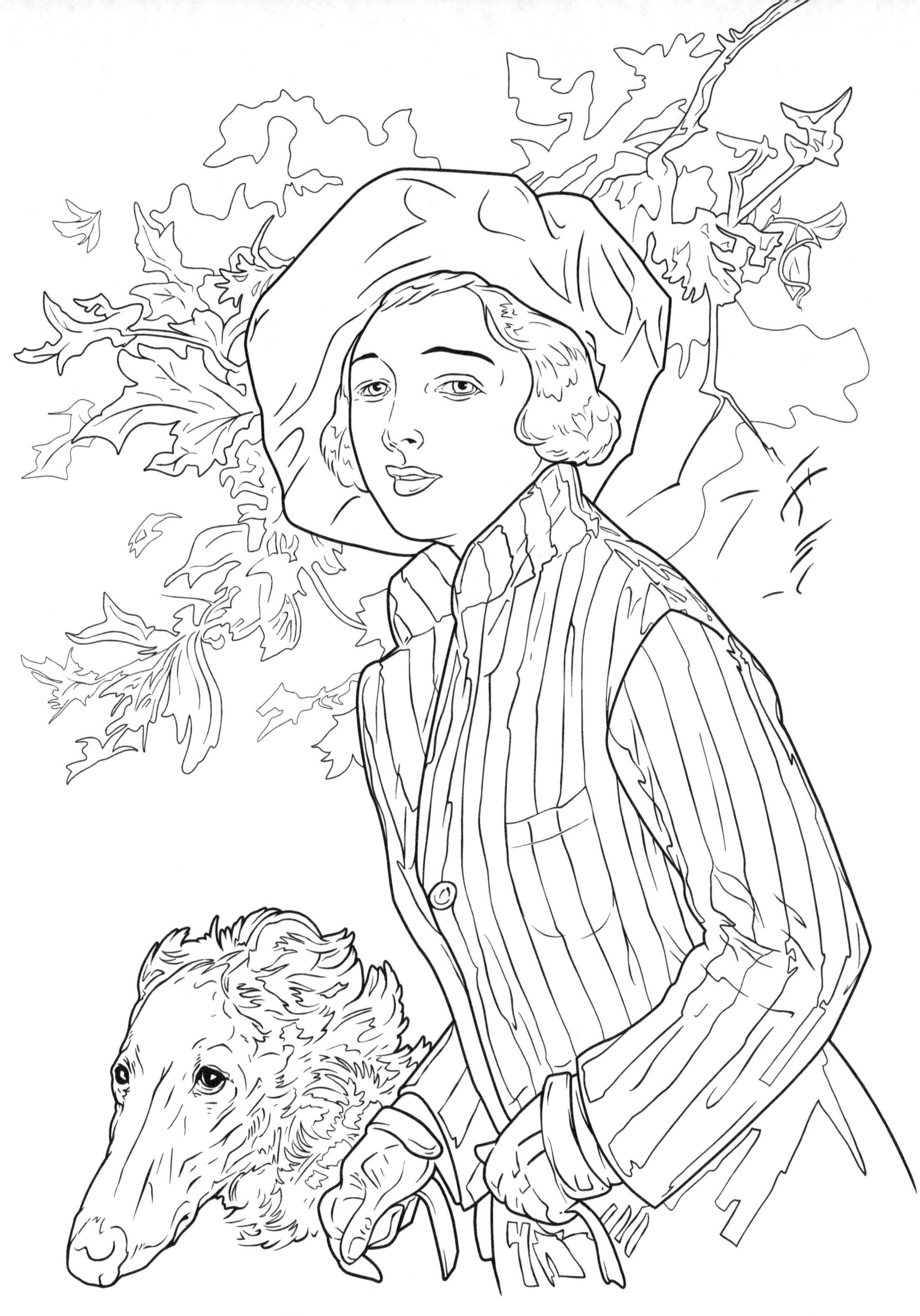

Harrison Fisher – 1917. *Woman with borzoi.*

© Diner Mighty

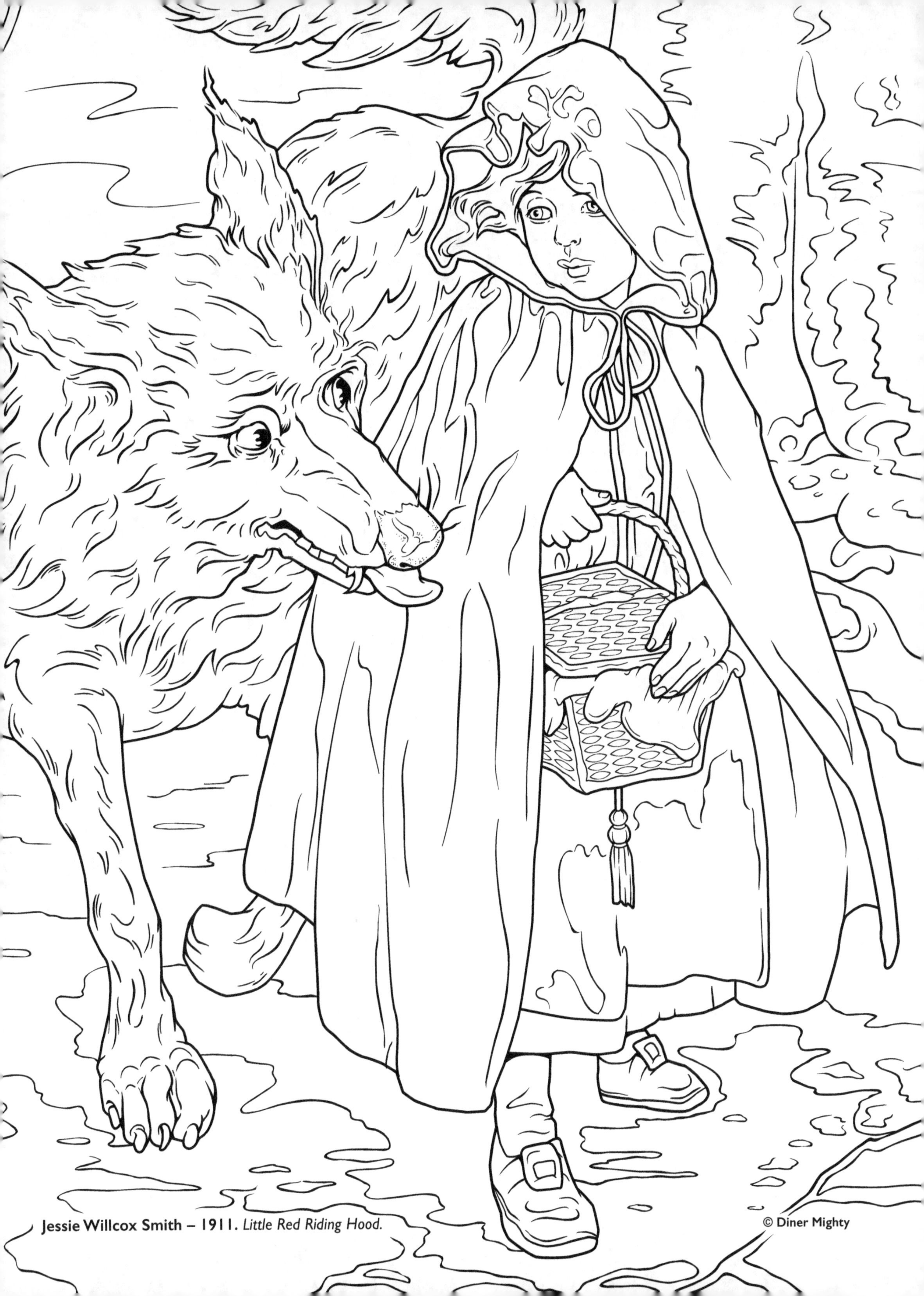

Jessie Willcox Smith – 1911. *Little Red Riding Hood.*

© Diner Mighty

J.C. Leyendecker – 1923. Arrow Collar advertisement.
© Diner Mighty

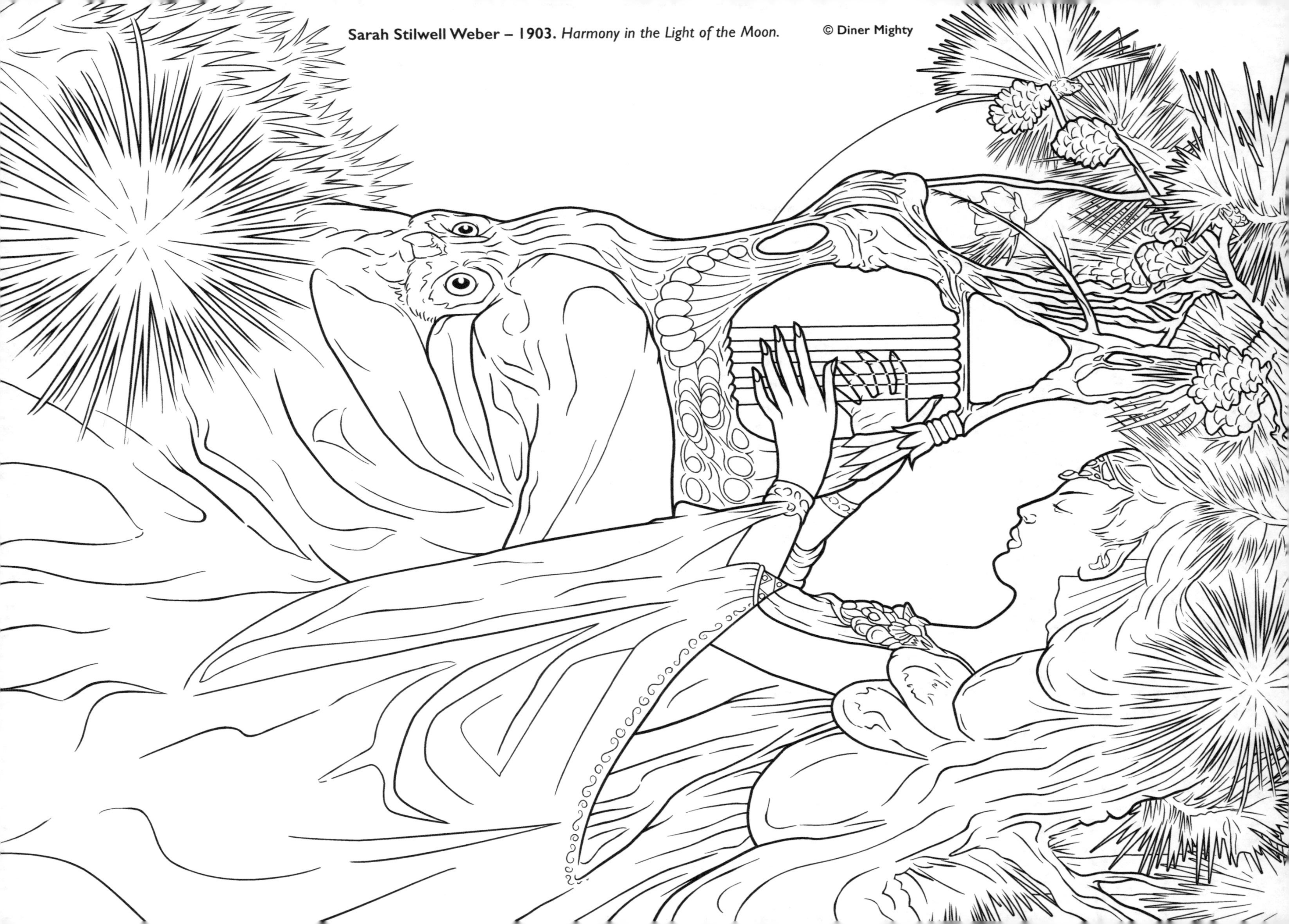

Sarah Stilwell Weber – 1903. Harmony in the Light of the Moon.
© Diner Mighty

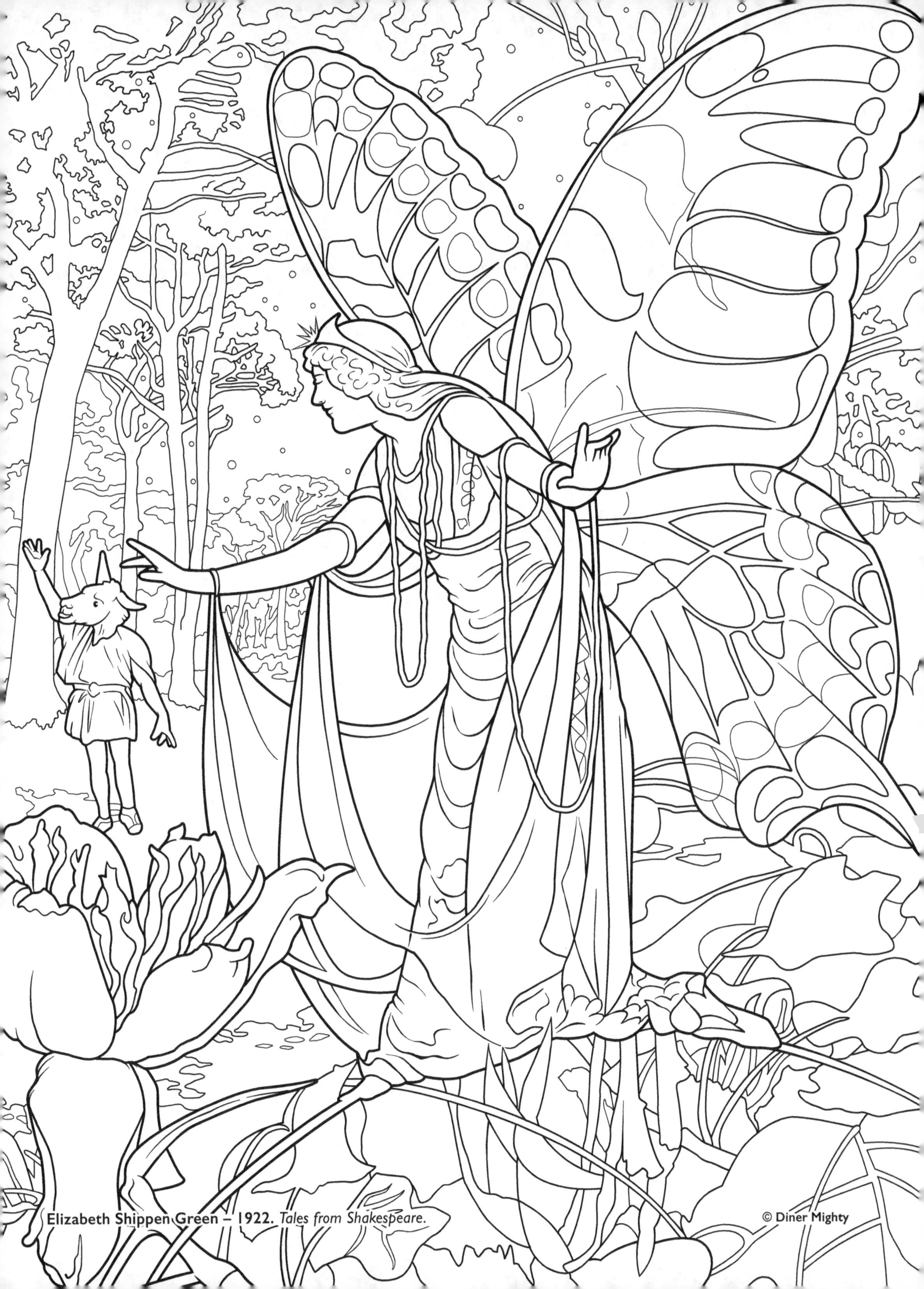
Elizabeth Shippen Green – 1922. Tales from Shakespeare.
© Diner Mighty

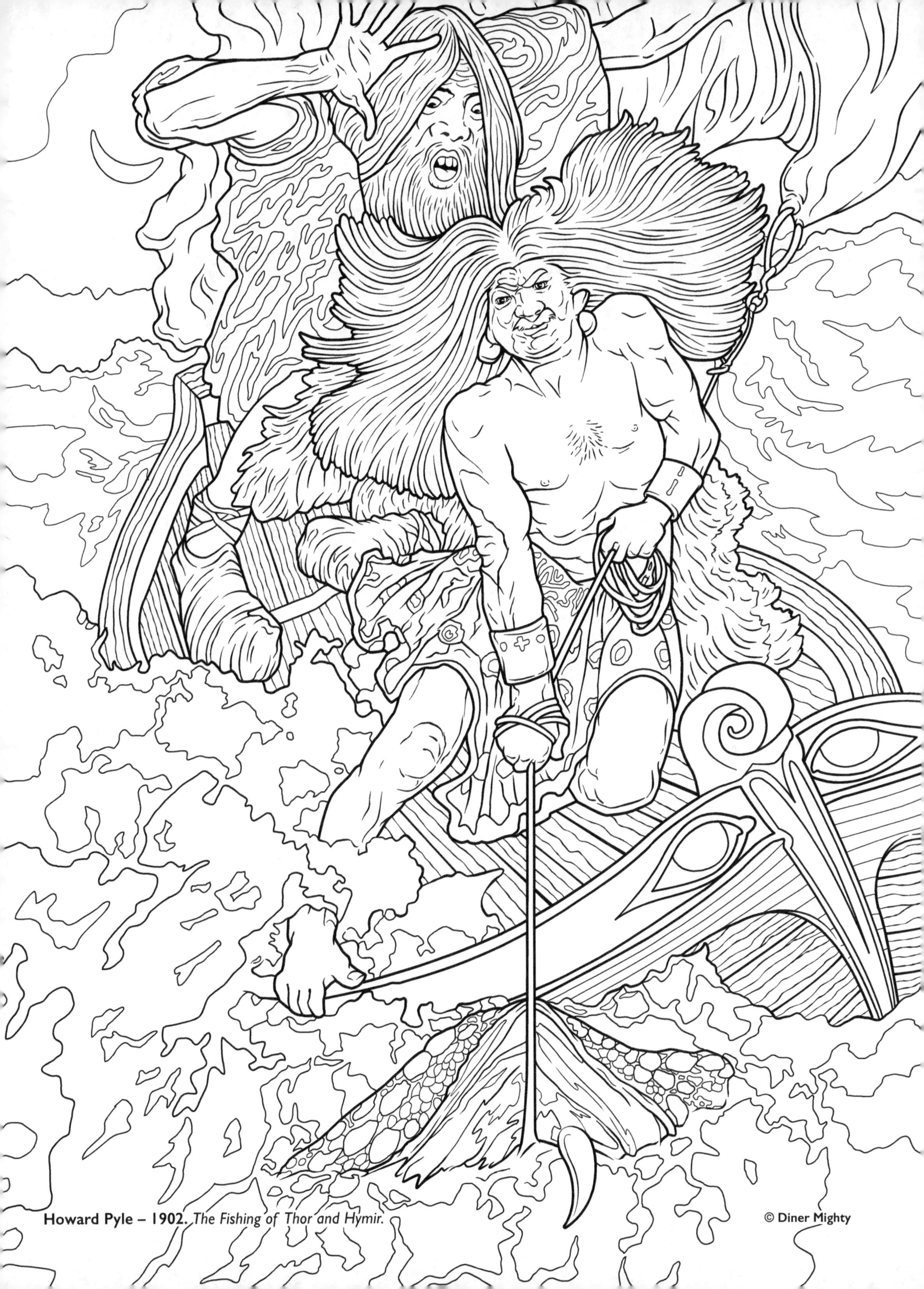

Howard Pyle – 1902. *The Fishing of Thor and Hymir.*

© Diner Mighty

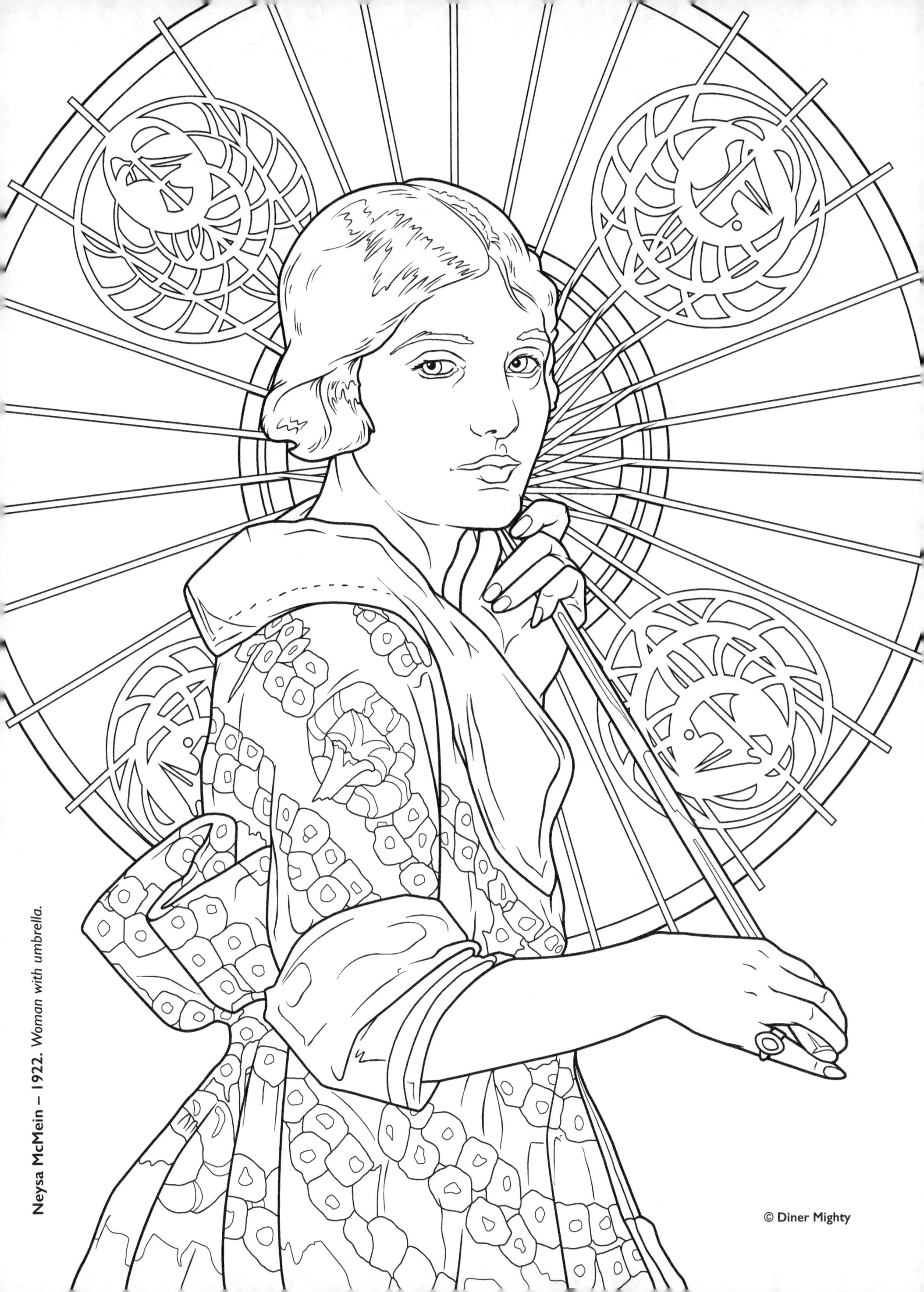

Neysa McMein – 1922. Woman with umbrella.
© Diner Mighty

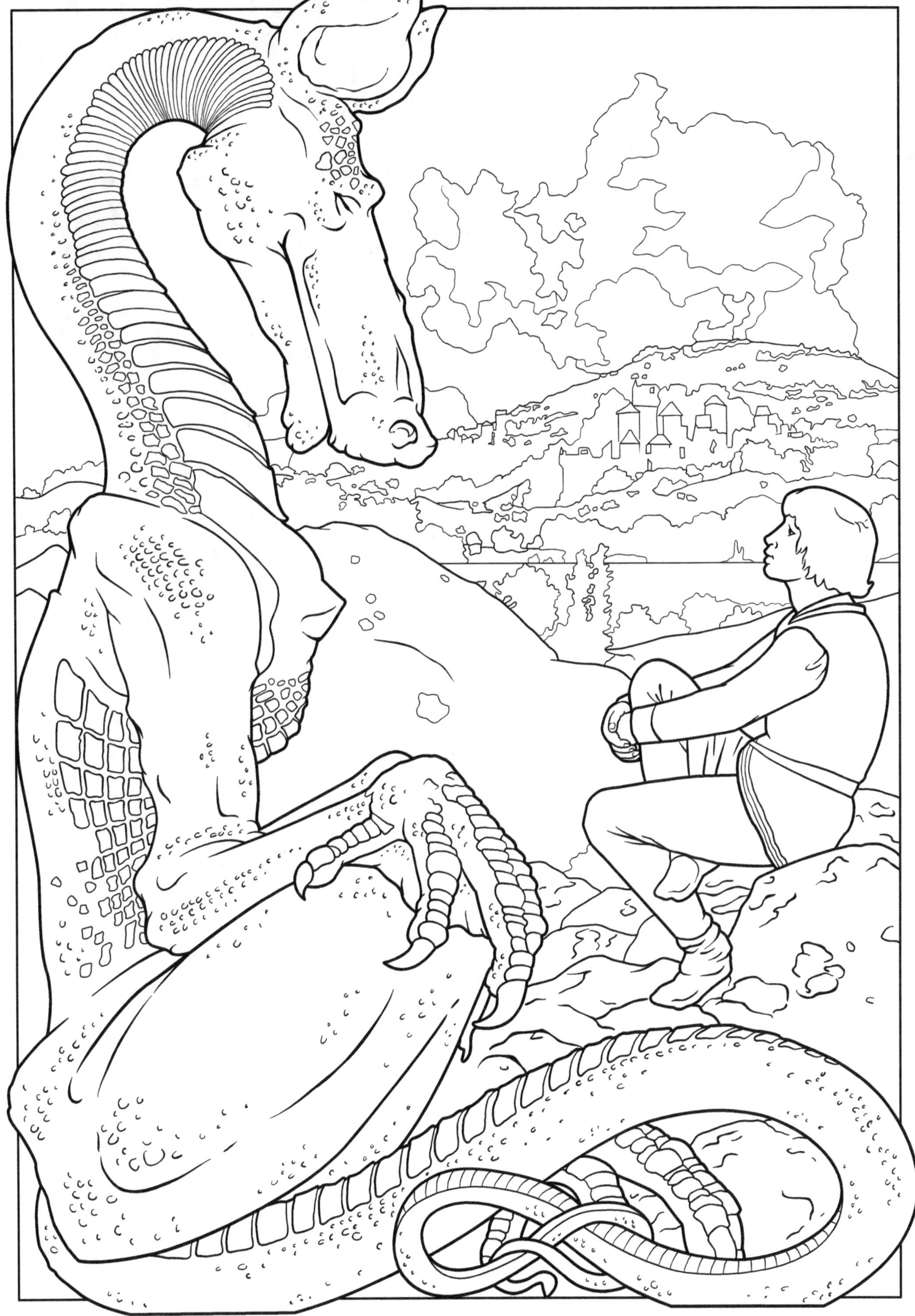

Maxfield Parrish – 1901. *The Reluctant Dragon.*